SEEING GOD THROUGH THE HUMAN BODY

A Doctor's Meditation on the Human Miracle
2nd Edition

SEEING GOD THROUGH THE HUMAN BODY

*A Doctor's Meditation
on the Human Miracle*
2nd Edition

Dr Robert Peprah-Gyamfi

THANK YOU JESUS BOOK

SEEING GOD THROUGH THE HUMAN BODY-
A Doctor's Meditation on the Human Miracle
2nd Edition
First published in 2009 by High Way
A division of Anomalos Publishing House, Crane , MO 65633, USA

Published by Thank You Jesus Books

For information please email:
tyjb@peprah-gyamfi.com

www.peprah-gyamfi.com

ISBN: 978-0-9955524-3-2

All scripture references are from the King James Version.

To all preachers of the Gospel of Christ Jesus the Righteous One, that they may preach the Word boldly without fear or favour of mortal man.

I will praise thee; for I am fearfully and wonderfully made:
marvellous are thy works; and that my soul knoweth right well.
—Psalm 139:14

Contents

Foreword to 2nd Edition

M uch has changed in the world since I put a full stop to my manuscript a little over eight years ago.

On the personal front, much as I would have liked to have kept my deep black hair which adorned my head in 2009 up to this day, my body physiology is not performing in the way I would like. Instead, I have watched helplessly as grey hairs have set in – not only set in, but also encroached upon the black which has struggled to keep pace with the rate at which the new, and without doubt domineering newcomer is going about its business.

It is not just my hair that is greying! Looking into the mirror these days, I have noticed my face is losing its elasticity; lines and wrinkles are appearing; forehead lines are deepening; the skin looks loose and tired and the temples appear sunken.

Back in 2009, my body physiology was happily able to cope with the mostly twelve-hour-a-day, six-days-a-week work pattern I was used to. But no more, it seems!

Though I am inclined even to this day to, as it were, forcefully impose that work schedule on my body, I have all too often realised to my dismay that, unlike previous times, my body struggles to make a recovery whenever it is made to undergo the ordeal. Indeed, my physiology is becoming weaker and weaker by the day, and whether

I like it or not, mortal man that I am, the signs are slowly but surely pointing towards the inevitable end.

On the family level, I have watched our three children grow, from kids and teenagers into adolescence and adulthood. The eldest of the three has indeed moved away to experience life outside the realm of parental control.

My wife on her part does all she can to, as it were, beat the ageing process. Whether she has succeeded in doing so or not will not be revealed to the reader.

Comparing the world of 2009 to that of 2017, my impression – I may be wrong – is that life on planet earth which has been unstable ever since our first parents rebelled against our Creator, has become even more unstable in recent times.

When I was seated at my desk in 2009 reflecting on the mystery of the human body, I could not imagine a time could come when an elected president of the United States would question the relevance of NATO. Well, events of the recent past have shown that I was far from right in my assumption.

Not only, at least from my perspective, has the world of 2009 become more uncertain compared to today's world, it has also become a lot more dangerous.

For example, whenever I left my home in 2009 to travel to London, about 160 kilometres to the south, I was never concerned that someone could, out of the blue, deliberately drive his vehicle onto the pavement with the intention of sending me and other pedestrians to a gruesome end. Recent events have evoked in me a certain degree of apprehension whenever I happen to be on my feet, not only on the streets of the British and Commonwealth capital but also on the streets of other major cities in the British Isles – and indeed elsewhere in Europe.

I do not have the statistics, but over the last nine years, hundreds of thousands, if not millions, have said farewell to planet earth, either through natural means or violent circumstances.

In keeping with the Twi saying "the road to the unknown is not a one-way street," the world has not only lost sons and daughters but also welcomed new arrivals. Indeed, while a large number of world residents have departed the world arena since 2009, an equally large, if not significantly larger, number of new arrivals have made planet earth their new home.

No doubt a good many of those who left the scene have held tenaciously to the belief that there is no God, even denied to their very last breaths the existence of God.

In the same vein, quite a good many of the new arrivals during the period under consideration, the late-comers to the world stage one might call them, will in the course of their stay here challenge the existence of God Almighty.

Despite the changes in my personal and family fortunes, pleasant and unpleasant; despite the stormy and turbulent times of the present world; despite the disasters and catastrophes of the world – natural and man-made – indeed, in spite of the economic, political, social and all other upheavals we hear, see and read about in our day, one thing has not changed as far as I am concerned – my firm conviction that the human body is not the result of a combination of a chain of chance events in a process called evolution. Consider the brain that gives us thought; the ears that help us hear the news of the day, good and bad; the eyes that help us see our environment – the beautiful roses, the boundless oceans, the mighty elephants; the heart that dutifully pumps blood to nourish our body systems and in so doing keeps us alive, etc., etc. – can all this intricate, all this elaborate, indeed all this complex intelligent design be the result of sheer coincidence, indeed the result of natural selection changing species through evolution driven my chance!

Indeed, while I do not have the answers to all the things that happen around me, for example why one would go to the extent of inflicting the most horrific pain to one's body in an act of suicide bombing and in the process sending innocent bystanders to their gruesome and premature deaths, there is one thing I am convinced of and to which I will hold steadfastly to my very last breath! This is my conviction that I can see the hand of Almighty God the Creator of Heaven and Earth at work in my body, every blessed day of my life – from waking up in the morning, engaging in my personal daily hygiene in the bathroom, sitting down to enjoy my breakfast, engaging in my daily chores and activities, retiring to bed after a tedious day's work, then lost in mysterious sleep and waking up refreshed to begin a new day.

My only wish is that when the time comes and I lie on my bed awaiting the final call, as my personal clock of time ticks out the minutes before the final midnight hour, that I will be able to garner enough strength in my faculties to declare for the very, very, final time with the Psalmist:

I will praise thee; for I am fearfully and wonderfully made: marvellous are thy works; and that my soul knoweth right well.

—Psalm 139:14

To His Name be the Glory, Now and Forevermore – Amen.

Dr Robert Peprah-Gyamfi
Loughborough, Leicestershire
UK

Foreword to 1st Edition

W hen I attended my first year Zoology course at the University of Natal way back in 1962, the distinguished-looking professor surprised the students by climbing onto a table at the front of the lecture theatre. He assumed a crouching position on all fours. "This is how we walked about a long time ago," he announced. He transferred his weight to his feet and stood in a crouching position. "This is how we stood up many years later, like the gorillas," he continued. Gradually, he became more erect. "Later, like the Neanderthal man, we were nearly erect," he said, before assuming his normal erect position. "This," he said, "is how we became human—through a long process of evolution, as a result of countless mutations and natural selection. You need to remember this, since it is fundamental to all you are going to learn in Zoology."

I was shocked. I knew all about Darwin's theory of evolution, of course, and, like Charles Kingsley, the Victorian author, even considered it feasible as the method God chose to create Humankind, conceding that God might well have meant the account in Genesis as a parable of the creation process. I never expected people to present the theory as fact and Gospel truth—especially in a university course!

So many years later, now, in 2008, I am equally surprised, pleasantly so, to find the Creationists are gaining ground, in spite of the audacity of scientists like Professor Dawkins who, in his TV series, unashamedly denies the existence of a Divine Designer.

Dr. Robert Peprah-Gyamfi is a Creationist par excellence! It is indeed gratifying that a medical doctor like Dr. Peprah-Gyamfi should use his leanings and insights as a doctor to make the case for Creationism, which gives the Lord Almighty full credit for the creation of humankind as recorded in the Bible. Having read his book, I have to yield to the clear evidence of a Divine Creator—I can see no reason why any readers will not perceive for themselves the incredible uniqueness of the intelligence that has surely gone into the various systems that keep the human body alive and functioning. The brain, heart, liver, kidneys, spine—all of these and many more could only have come about through remarkably clever forethought and planning.

What is more, every human being, unlike the animals that some believe gave rise to human beings, is remarkably unique, which again shows the hand of God. "There are no ordinary people," C. S. Lewis wrote. "You have never talked to a mere mortal." And it's true—each one of us is God's special creation. Unbelievably, no one else is just like you or me. Your physical appearance, your voice, your personality traits—all these make you one of a kind. Even your fingerprints distinguish you from any other human being.

Further, each one of us is valuable to God, made in his own image, every hair on our heads numbered. We are, as Dr. Peprah-Gyamfi says quoting the psalmist, "fearfully and wonderfully made" (Ps. 139:14). The human body, without exaggeration, is a miracle, or better still, the sum total of miracles. Indeed, there are thousands upon thousands, if not millions upon millions or billions upon billions of miracles simultaneously at work in our bodies to keep us going.

Appealing to common sense and drawing upon his medical knowledge, the author lays bare the sheer wonder of our design.

Thinking men and women will surely see that what he reveals is true, that behind it all is a loving and patient Creator who sustains us, even the atheist who denies Him. The fact is we are precious to God, who continues to love us even when we pay him no mind, even when we deny his existence.

Charles Muller, MA (Wales), PhD (London),
D.Litt (OFS), D.Ed (SA)

Acknowledgments

My thanks go to God Almighty, Creator of heaven and earth, for the impartation of wisdom needed to write this book. Rita, my wife, together with our children Karen, David, and Jonathan, also deserve my thanks and appreciation for their support and encouragement to successfully conclude this work.

I am also grateful to Dr. Charles Muller of Diadembooks.com for carrying out the initial editorial work on the manuscript and for writing the Foreword to the first edition.

Finally, I am deeply indebted to Dr. Hugh Mann for his permission to quote from his article "What is common sense?" published on his website OrganicMD.org.

Introduction
A Matter of Common Sense

D uring my time at medical school in Germany, my heart was constantly aggrieved when one lecturer after the other—be it in Anatomy, Biochemistry, or Physiology—gave credit to the "god" evolution, backed by his agent natural selection or the "goddess" Mother Nature, for the creation of life on earth, the creation of the human race. Yes, men of letters gave glory to evolution and/or Mother Nature for bringing about the human body and all the complicated organs it contains.

Not only on the macroscopic plane of human existence did evolution and Mother Nature receive glory for these astounding achievements; they also singled them out for praise in the realm of the microscopic as well. For example, when we considered the cell, the unit of life, and dwelt on its complex structure and the incredibly intricate yet orderly reactions occurring within it, again the party responsible for everything was evolution, natural selection, Mother Nature.

As I soon learned, my lecturers' thinking could not be regarded as isolated, as representing a point of view confined to the walls of institutions of higher learning, but rather reflected the thinking of a considerable proportion of the German population.

I have in the meantime moved from Germany to the UK. As I soon realised, the situation on the British Isles with regard to this issue is no better than that in the country of Goethe and Schiller. I have in the meantime concluded—perhaps I am wrong—that a considerable proportion of the Western World and the countries of the former Eastern Block, including China, to explain the origin of life on earth, adhere to the concept of chance evolution as proposed by Charles Darwin and later refined by his admirers.

As a reflection of the widespread denial of the existence of God Almighty in the world in our day, there has been a surge in literature that aims to not only challenge the established truths of the Church of Jesus Christ my Lord, but also to seek to deny completely the existence of God.

Below are just a few examples of the numerous atheistic books I found on sale on the internet:

The Da Vinci Code (Dan Brown)
Atheistic Universe (David Mills)
Atheism: The Case Against God (George Smith)
The God Delusion (Professor Dawkins)

The Da Vinci Code and *The God Delusion* have sold over one million copies each.

Among those who contributed to the number, without doubt, are those who, although they hold views opposite to those expressed by the authors, still chose to obtain copies in order to equip themselves with the needed ammunition to challenge the views of the authors. I dare say with all certainty, however, that the overwhelming majority of those who purchased copies did so because they were either declared atheists or persons who sympathized with their cause.

Although I found such blatant disrespect for the Living God of heaven and earth appalling, for a while I remained quiet. In the first place, I did not want to create the impression of wanting to fight God's fight for Him. Indeed, I do believe in the ability of the Almighty God I serve to fight His own fight in His own way and in His own time.

In this regard, I find it difficult coming to terms with the adherents of a religion, the name of which I do not wish to mention, who create the impression that they have to fight personally to defend their religion. When I see adherents of that religion on TV wielding swords and machetes, threatening to tear to pieces the bodies of those they regard as having insulted the dignity of their religion, I wonder why they feel the need to go to such lengths, resorting even to violence. At best, let words—the power of argument—fight your fight, not force or the threat thereof.

No, I do not believe in the use of force to challenge a person like Professor Dawkins, the title of whose book, *The God Delusion*, creates the impression that a person like myself who holds one hundred percent to the existence of the Lord of Hosts has lost his mind—indeed, a case for psychiatric treatment.

My belief in non-violence as a way of confronting the honourable man of letters is inspired by the way and manner in which the Lord Jesus Christ Himself dealt with His enemies. For example, when the mob went to arrest Him the night before His crucifixion, Peter, one of His disciples, drew his sword and cut off the ear of the High Priest's servant who was one of those sent to arrest Him (John18:10–11; Luke 22:50–51). In considering the circumstances surrounding the incident, the heart of sinful man is apt to shout: "Hooray! It serves you right! You came to arrest and torture Peter's Master. You wanted to get at his Master—now Peter has got at you! That has nothing to do with an eye for an eye; no, it is purely a matter of self defence—nothing wrong with that!"

The onlookers, perhaps even those there to arrest Him, had probably expected the Lord to applaud Peter for fighting on His side, or at least to remain neutral and concentrate on issues relating to the appropriate strategy for saving His own skin. Instead, to the utter amazement of those present, He picks up the ear and replaces it—the wound instantly healed. Goodwill towards your enemy when he or she aims at your heart: absolutely incredible.

Still, I have decided not to keep quiet, but to respond in my own way to the increasing spread of atheism in our world. In pondering my response to the issue, it became clear to me that as far as hardcore atheists, including the above-named authors are concerned, there is not much I can achieve by way of counter-argument or direct persuasion—so convinced are they in their stance. Yes, I have decided to put arguments aside.

Instead, I have resolved to resort to the power of prayer—to employ the grace and mercy of the gracious and merciful God in their lives. I am encouraged in this respect by the life of Saul of Tarsus who became the great apostle Paul. In the same way, the atheists of our day go about persecuting the Church of Christ, my Lord Himself you might say, by way of their books and lectures.

Saul of Tarsus, in his time, persecuted the Church of Christ with incredible ferocity. Then it happened. One day, as Saul was on his way to Damascus on a mission geared towards further persecution of the Church of Christ the Redeemer, the Big Boss Himself confronted the man of mere flesh. Soon, Saul, the persecutor, became Paul, Soldier of the Cross. Indeed, with God all things are possible.

In the case of the renowned champions of atheism, I have resorted to prayer to bring change. But when it comes to the ordinary teeming millions, individuals unsurprisingly confused by the conflicting signals reaching them from all angles, I have decided to intervene in the form of a book I hope will point the way to the God of heaven and earth.

In what better way can a medical doctor contribute to the debate than by way of an area of study quite familiar to him—the human body? Indeed, there are so many miracles taking place in our body, miracles that point to the hand of an Intelligent Designer, that as far as I am concerned it is superfluous to look elsewhere for proof of the existence of God Almighty.

I intend this book to appeal to common sense. What is common sense? To find an answer to the question, I consulted the Internet. After typing in the term in a popular search engine, the following definitions cropped up:

1. Sound and prudent judgement based on a simple perception of the situation or facts[1]
2. Practical judgment that is independent of specialized knowledge, training, or the like; normal native intelligence[2]
3. Practical good sense[3]

One can describe common sense as the basic sense our Creator placed in us, which enables us to cope with the basic challenges of life. It is that sense, for example, that enabled our uneducated ancestors to go about their daily lives on the planet onto which the Almighty had placed them.

Education may refine our thinking, but even without education we can rely on our common sense to help us arrive at a sound judgment in a matter, even though we do not possess specialized knowledge in that field of human endeavour. For example, we do not require a PhD in physics or mechanical engineering to figure out that when we

1. Merriam-Webster Online. http://www.merriam-webster.com/dictionary/common sense
2. Dictionary.com Unabridged (v 1.1). Random House, Inc. http://dictionary.reference.com/ browse/common sense
3. Kernerman English Multilingual Dictionary. K Dictionaries Ltd. http://dictionary.reference.com/browse/common sense

stand before a vehicle set in motion and heading in our direction it will knock us down and inflict injuries to our bodies: bones, muscles, internal organs—injuries that might well result in our death.

The engineer, the physicist, the expert in matters of dynamics, may want to know the mass of the vehicle and the speed at which it was travelling at the time of impact with our bodies to calculate the force with which it crushed them into pieces. What use will that be to us as we lie under the wheels of the truck, screaming in excruciating pain, assuming we managed to survive the collision in the first place?

What does common sense tell us to do before we get ourselves into that precarious situation? Good friend, I advise you to take to your heels and escape the danger while you can!

In the process of browsing the Web for material related to the issue of common sense, I came across a passage that not only gave me food for thought on the matter, but served as a good reflection of the message my book seeks to convey. With the kind permission of the author, Dr. Hugh Mann of OrganicMD.org, I have reproduced the passage in its entirety:

> I learned the lesson of common sense as a third-year medical student. I was doing an internal medicine rotation at a Veterans Affairs (VA) hospital and working with interns, residents, and attending physicians. One day, on morning rounds, we examined a patient with a black tongue. The intern assigned to that patient had researched all the causes of a black tongue and was eager to demonstrate his new knowledge.
>
> As the intern started to lecture us, the attending physician interrupted him and asked the patient if he uses black cough drops. The patient smiled, opened the drawer of his night table, and took out a package of Smith Brothers black cough drops.

The intern's face turned red, and we all laughed. The intern was so focused on being a doctor that he forgot to ask his patient an obvious question. It's been thirty-five years since I was a third-year medical student, but I still have a vivid memory of that day and that lesson: use common sense and pay attention to the obvious.

My thirty years of medical practice have taught me the lesson of common sense again and again. Eventually, I realised that society in general, and modern medicine in particular, lack common sense. This is why societal and medical problems are rarely solved. Let's apply common sense to health-care.

Use common sense and pay attention to the obvious. How true is the wisdom inherent in that sentence? In my opinion, when it comes to the issue of how our universe, including all that is contained in it, came into existence, we need only common sense to guide us to the truth. Oh, how many today are busily going about in search of complicated answers to the matter instead of accepting the truth as told by the Bible!

We may indeed disagree or differ as to the right path to Almighty God, Creator of heaven and earth; but to deny completely He exists amounts in my mind to closing our eyes to reality. Unfortunately, that is exactly what millions of human beings the world over continue to do.

Like the would-be doctor in the above passage, many in our day try to manufacture complicated theories, theses, conjectures, etc., to explain how our world came into being, when, in my opinion, we can arrive at a sound judgement just by considering ourselves, the way our own bodies are built. It is simple: we can retreat to the secret of our rooms. Alone with ourselves, we can expose ourselves, naked, the same way we arrived in the world years ago. We can then begin to wrestle with our own self. One by one, we can begin to test our own common sense. We could begin with our head—consider the hairs on our head, our head itself, our two eyes and two ears; our nose and how it sits wonderfully in the middle of our face; our mouth, our tongue, our teeth, our two hands, our two legs.

Next, we could begin to ponder, one after the other, all of our body parts and the way God structured them to perform their assigned functions.

Yes, for a moment let us withdraw from everything else to spend quiet time with ourselves. For the event, we must forget everything else, the cares and worries that plague us: debt, unemployment, marriage concerns, our children, world issues, politics, war, and rumours of war.

After we have been alone awhile with ourselves, let us ask ourselves, could we have come about because of pure chance? How could this be? We should keep reflecting. Could chance engineer such a perfect construction?

Indeed, many of us are looking for complicated answers to the matter of our existence instead of paying attention to the obvious. In this instance, we can cite Mr. Charles Darwin as a typical example.

In 1831, about 1,800 years after the God of heaven and earth had manifested Himself in the most powerful terms through His Son Jesus Christ my Lord and Redeemer, the honourable English gentleman, then twenty-two years of age, set sail with a ship called the *HMS Beagle* and headed for distant lands. He was on an expedition to find clues and answers to what remained a mystery to him: the origin of life.

You and I, let us ponder this. Nearly two thousand years after the Lord of creation walked the surface of the earth and displayed His creative power in the most powerful terms—feeding five thousand people from a few loaves of bread and a few fishes; turning water into wine; stilling boisterous waves by the raising of His arms and the mere command, "Peace, be still" (Mark 4:39); and restoring life into the decomposing body of Lazarus—the young Mr. Charles Darwin, only twenty-two years on planet earth, set out to find clues to the origin of life!

Satan and the host of his fallen angels, without doubt, were flabbergasted. "Here, at long last, is a brave young man who is not only prepared to challenge the established faith by word of mouth, but also through concrete action. Come on! Let us offer him all the assistance he may need," Satan exclaimed, his delight barely concealed.

The Great Deceiver assisted the naturalist in his declared aim. After experimenting, researching, experimenting, and re-researching (that gentleman must indeed have invested an incredible amount of energy in his endeavour), he discovered what he had gone out in search of—the secret behind the origin of life! In 1859, he published his findings in his book *The Origin of Species*. In it, he concluded that all species of life originated from a common ancestor, a primordial cell. Natural selection, he continued, assisted the process of evolution. Suddenly, Mr. Charles Darwin made my Lord the Righteous One look like a liar. Indeed, he urged everyone to throw overboard the revealed truth of creation through Almighty God.

As is usually the case with humanity, his proposition earned enthusiastic adherents. Even today, millions hold on to it.

While admitting that his studies led to considerable insight in several areas of creation, as far as I am concerned, his conclusion—namely, that life in the universe came about through sheer chance—is pure rubbish.

If you happen to be a brilliant chemist or food specialist and you succeed in cracking the formula behind Coca Cola, does that give you licence to deny that someone put the formula together in the first place?

Dear reader, if you happen to be a specialist in the area of computer software and you manage to crack the secret behind the workings of Microsoft Windows, would that lead you to conclude the engineers at Microsoft did not put the formula together in the first place?

Dear members of the jury, does the fact that the bucket I used as a child to fetch water from the Nwi River was made of aluminium, make it an airplane because the body of an airplane is also made of aluminium?

I shake my head in disbelief when some scientists in our day begin to boast and expect us to worship them because they have been able to crack the DNA code, the blueprint of life. You have cracked the code—and so what, friends? Does the human soul dwell within DNA?

God Almighty, whom I serve, placed the blueprint for the development of various forms of life in the structure we human beings call DNA. It is true that years of research have led humanity to gain insight into how DNA functions. But, does that give us licence to deny the existence of the Designer, He who put the structure in place to start with? Why do we seek to limit everything to the material plane of our existence, good friends, ladies and gentlemen?

As I indicated earlier, I will appeal to your common sense, dear reader. I want you to consider yourself a juror in the court of justice. I will present my case and leave you to decide for yourself based on common sense.

What, then, is the issue at stake? It goes to the very core of human existence; namely, how we came to be on planet earth in the first place.

There is a group of people, inspired by the likes of the late Mr. Charles Darwin and Professor Dawkins, one of the most vocal champions of atheism in contemporary times, who hold the view that there is no God. Yes, to this group of people the universe and all it contains came about through chance. You and I are mere matter, they claim. We live for a while and then die, and that is the end of us. To this group of people, life on the planet earth is meaningless. So, let us eat, drink, and be merry, for tomorrow we die!

If only the modern-day atheists would hold to their views and leave others to live their lives in peace. No! This group of people, increasingly, is becoming not only vocal but also gaining considerable influence in society. As we read above, some of them even have the audacity to state that anyone who believes in God Almighty are classified with the lunatics dwelling in Fantasy Land. Dear members of the jury, that is one side of the matter.

I, Kofi Peprah-Gyamfi, the village boy from little Mpintimpi in Ghana who during the course of my life adopted the European name Robert, completely ascribe to the biblical account that God Almighty, the I Am That I Am, Jehovah Jireh, the Loving One, the King of Kings and Lord of Lords, created the universe and everything including things seen and unseen in the universe.

The atheist might tell me I have compromised my position at the beginning of these legal proceedings by referring to the Holy Bible, a Book they do not believe in the first place.

Well, I do not buy their argument. Still, in order not to give them any cause to cry foul right at the outset, I am prepared, if even for a while, to keep the Bible out of the picture.

Indeed, should we decide even for awhile to cast aside the references to the workings of God in the Holy Bible and live in a world with no reference to the Holy Bible, no written account in regard to the work of the Divine—I still humbly submit that I see the work of the Divine Designer everywhere I go.

God's creation is huge. The evidence of the Divine confronts us everywhere we go. In fact, we could use several aspects of His creation to argue for His existence. Some, for example, may see in the botanical world, in the beautiful flowers around us, evidence of God's creation. Others may recognise in the order of the physical world evidence of the workings of a Higher Intelligence in the universe; still others may see in the biochemical reactions taking place in the living cell strong evidence for the workings of God in the universe.

I, however, have decided to restrict myself to the human body in my argument for Intelligent Design. I have several reasons for my decision. First, the Bible teaches that human beings are the climax of God's creation. What aspect of His handiwork is better suited as evidence of His ingenuity than the climax of His master creation?

Secondly, I have chosen to use the human body in my presentation because it is familiar to us all. We may be in the dark when it comes to the details of how individual bodily organs function. We may be unaware of the complexity of the human eye, but when we walk on the street and suddenly, for reasons best known to us, close our eyes and moments later hear the screeching of car tires that have stopped only centimetres away, we begin to appreciate how necessary eyes are to our survival. The same can be said of other parts of our body— our ears, our thumbs, our feet, etc.

Finally, I have chosen the human body for practical reasons—it is a field of study with which I, as a medical doctor, am quite familiar. I do not claim to be the best or most brilliant of my peers. However, by virtue of my apprenticeship with those who have taken it upon themselves to help cure the diseases that have plagued humankind since our fall from grace, I am conversant with the build-up and functioning of the human body. This fact will enable me to present my case before you, the eminent jurors of the matter before us, with some degree of confidence.

Before I begin, I wish to reiterate my point: I want to appeal to your common sense, people of the jury. Do not be intimidated by the fact that you may not happen to hold a degree in Human Anatomy, Pathology, Physiology, Biochemistry, or Pharmacology. I will do my best to present the facts in a manner you can understand. I want you to avoid any preconceived notions and ideas with regard to the case before you. Instead, I entreat you to concentrate only on the facts and nothing but the facts.

Chapter 1
The Miracle of Life

I shall begin my discourse at the beginning of human existence, the point of conception. Though it has been terribly abused, horribly demeaned, awfully degraded; though a booming commercial industry has developed leading to the routine use of terms like *sex workers*, *single sex couples*, *bisexuals*, and *homosexuals*, I am deeply convinced that when He created Human sexual reproduction, God Almighty, Creator of heaven and earth, had only goodness at heart.

I sincerely believe that The Rock of Ages, He who called the universe into being, in line with His character, had well-meaning intentions when He chose to co-operate with Humanity in the multiplication of humankind. Rather than adopting a method whereby, as a way of propagating our race, causing us from time to time to break into two individuals as in cellular division, He instead developed a plan whereby two human beings, one complementing the other, became involved in the process. It is a plan beautiful in its originality and by no means boring.

Just as opposite poles of a magnetic field attract, Almighty God created two individuals whose features attracted each other. He intended this to be an exciting relationship, joy to the utmost that found its climax in the sexual act. Through the exciting, fulfilling experience, male sperm would unite with the female egg in conception. An offspring, in whom the parents would recognize each other, would result from the union. His or her birth would not only bring joy, but also deepen their bond.

The Lord looked and beheld the human pair He had created and saw that they were beautiful. "Therefore shall the man leave his father and his mother, and shall cleave unto his wife: and they shall be one flesh" (Gen. 2:24). This is the ideal plan hatched by the Lord of Hosts in the heaven of heavens. He intended marriage, the union of the two sexes, as a wonderful and fulfilling relationship. The picture of the family functioning properly was to be a reflection of heaven on earth.

By way of intensive study and research into the Creative Works of God Almighty, we have come to realise that He built our bodies of cells. Each cell contains chromosomes containing the information needed to perform various functions in the body. We now know each human cell contains twenty-three pairs of chromosomes. Now, I ask your attention, for I will soon reveal the ingenuity of the Master Creator! I hope that in recognizing and reflecting upon this you have no choice but to join me in bowing our heads in awe of the astounding wisdom of God our Creator.

As I mentioned earlier, our cells contain twenty-three chromosome pairs. If the Divine had decreed the propagation of the human race should be via the union of two complementary individuals—the female and male—on a cellular level, something essential had to happen. Failure to do so would jeopardise the undertaking, because a union of two human cells each containing twenty-three pairs of chromosomes would result in an offspring having forty-six pairs of chromosomes! Since the Divine had decreed that twenty-three pairs of chromosomes should unveil the mystery hidden within them and develop a healthy human being, the union would not lead to a human being, but something else.

The proponents of evolution would have a field day, for every stage of the union would lead to a different organism. The union of two human cells, each boasting twenty-three pairs of chromosomes, would give rise to an offspring possessing forty-six pairs of chromosomes— perhaps we could call them *Homo Sapiens Darwinicus* after the brilliant discoverer of chance evolution.

The next generation in the process would contain 184 chromosomes, to be known as *Homo Sapiens Atheisticus*, in honour of those who have denied the existence of their Creator or who will do so in the future. In the course of time, an offspring *Homo Sapiens Supermodernicus*, capable of flying straight to Mars, would come into being!

Since the design of I Am That I Am, the Big Boss of creation, since the purpose of Almighty God, the Loving and Good One, was to keep humans human, He devised a brilliant idea. Contrary to the lie those who hold to the concept of chance evolution broadcast, God Almighty whom I serve leaves nothing to chance. In fact, He who cares for the birds of the air and lilies of the field leaves nothing to accident. That is why He chose sexual reproduction as a means for propagating the human race.

To make sure human beings reproduced human beings, He decreed that the female egg and male sperm cells directly involved in the process of sexual reproduction should each have only one version of the twenty-three pairs of chromosomes needed to give rise to new individual. And so it was. Is it not amazing that even on the level of a microscopic unit such as the cell, the God I serve is in charge?

Ask those who make it their profession to study the cell on the microscopic level, and if they confess—if their pride allows them to confess—they will admit it is a mystery; indeed, the way things work even on the cellular plane is a mystery. We might regard the cell as a factory where numerous chemical reactions take place. The other day I read an article written by an eminent scientist. He went a step further to speak of the cell as the most complex factory on earth. I paused awhile to reflect on his assertion. I could consider a whole organ, the liver for example, as being the most complicated factory on earth—but to assign this accolade to the microscopic entity the cell is amazing! Remember, this is not a factory in which each unit functions arbitrarily. No, each component of the factory knows how to play its role perfectly, how to act in accordance with a blueprint in order to ensure the whole factory produces what is required of it. Come; join me in giving Almighty God some well-deserved applause!

Is it not beyond belief that of all the approximately 60 trillion cells that make up the human being, only the female eggs and male sperm are equipped with a single each of the twenty-three chromosomes which are otherwise found paired in other cells?[4] Even more fascinating, the twenty-three chromosomes have unique structures.

One could imagine that when the twenty-three chromosomes of the sperm meet the twenty-three chromosomes from the egg, they would arbitrarily align themselves. No, contrary to the confused state in which humanity has left the planet assigned to it, the God of creation is not a God of confusion but a God of order and love. He gave the chromosomes from each parent the capability to align themselves with their match.

As an illustration: egg chromosome A searches for and locates chromosome A from the sperm; in the same way, chromosome B from the egg finds chromosome B from the sperm, and so it goes until all twenty-three pairs are aligned.

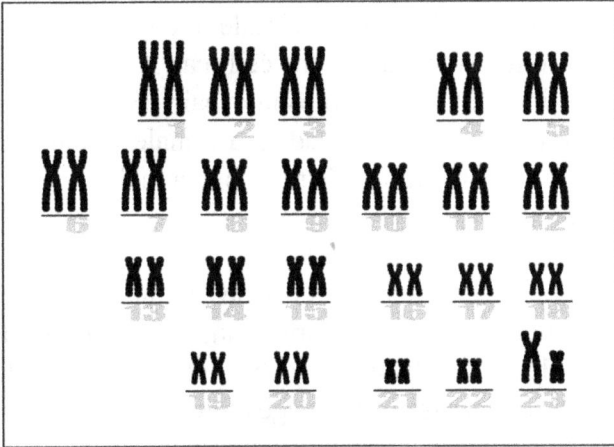

Fig.1A. Human Chromosomes Male(23XY)

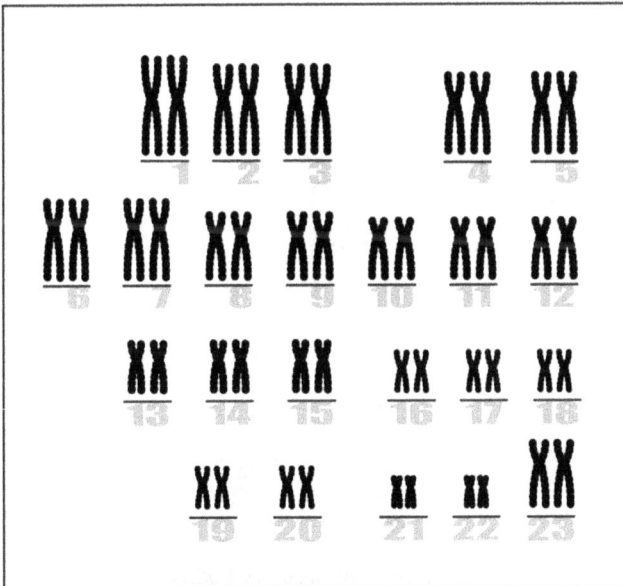

Fig.1B. Female(23XX)

5

Even here, Almighty God did not leave matters to chance. As we noted earlier, He created male and female to complement each other. The first 22 chromosome pairs in the cell play no role in determining the sex of an individual. Chromosome pair 23 assumes this role. These X- and Y-chromosomes lead to a female in the combination XX, whereas the combination XY results in a male.

It is yet another mystery!

The cells of the body are continually dividing. Not only do the cells that produce sperm and eggs divide, but also so do the normal body cells, including those that form skin, hair, and muscles. When body cells divide, two cells result, each containing twenty-three pairs of chromosomes. There is no exchange of genetic material when such a division occurs.

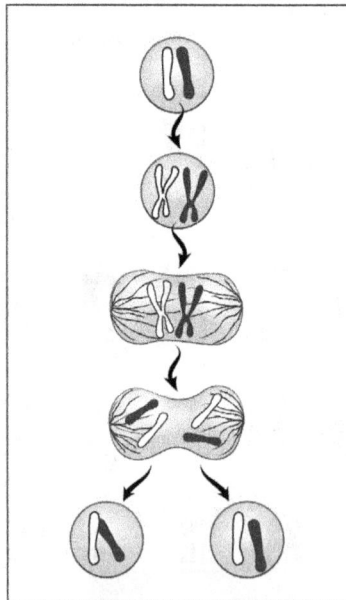

Fig. 2. Division of ordinary bodily cells.

On the other hand, when the original cells, which serve as a factory for the production of sperm and eggs, divide, something extraordinary happens. The primary spermatocytes (for the male) and the primary egg cell (for the female) like any other cell in the body contain twenty-three chromosome pairs. However, in this exceptional case, each of these cells undergoes a series of divisions that result in four cells, each containing only a single each of the twenty-three human chromosomes.

Why is there such a terrific exception to the general rule in this particular instance?

Let us ponder yet another wonder surrounding the concept of human sexual reproduction. This is something you might not be aware of, or perhaps you are aware of it but have until now not given it much thought. We know that the semen a male ejaculates during a sexual act contains on average about 200 million sperm. Incredible, isn't it? Take a moment to consider that this is an amount of sperm that could in theory give rise to about two-thirds of the population of the United States (based on July 2007 figures).

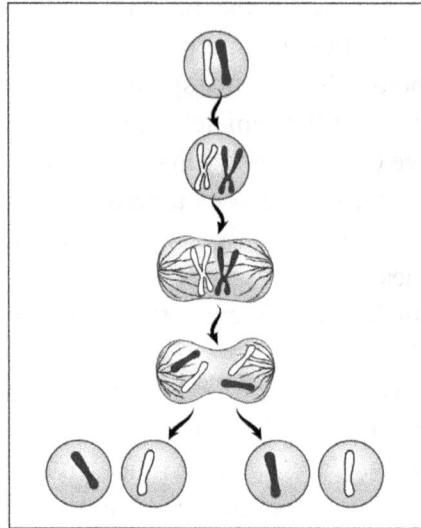

Fig. 3. Contrary to the situation found in the bodily cells, when the cells responsible for sperm and egg production divide, four cells result, each containing only a single each of the 23 human chromosomes.

But wait, friend; you may become even more astounded. As I mentioned earlier, forming a human being requires twenty-three pairs of chromosomes. During each menstrual cycle, a woman usually releases only one egg, though there are occasional exceptions to the rule when a female releases more than one egg. For the present discussion, however, we will use the norm.

Let us imagine 200 million active sperm competing to fertilise *one* egg! Ponder it: 200 million sperm offered the chance to penetrate a single egg in a small, enclosed space. We could think of 200 million individuals aiming 200 million arrows at an object a few centimetres away. I do not count myself as one of the sharpshooters of our race; nevertheless, given a bow and arrow and asked to hit a target a few centimetres away, I am certain to hit the mark. Even if I do not, there will certainly be several trained sharpshooters within the huge number capable of hitting the target.

In the same way, we would expect several sperm among the huge number discharged by the would-be father to succeed in penetrating the egg simultaneously to fertilise it.

We will take a cautiously moderate approach to the matter. After all, some of the 200 million sperm might collide with one another and become incapacitated; others, as slow as tortoises, give up the race along the way. Still others, weak and fragile, might be crushed by the masses—so we might assume a mere ninety-nine sperm out of the original 200 million will succeed in hitting the mark, and with such ferocity as to permit their penetration of the egg to bring about fertilisation! That would lead to the transfer of 2,277 chromosomes to the egg. Add to that the twenty-three chromosomes already in the egg and we come up with a fertilised egg containing 2,300 chromosomes.

Such creations would lead not to ordinary human beings like you and me, but something else—a being of unimaginable capability and intelligence, a being capable of existing under the conditions prevailing on the sun. In light of this, those holding to the belief that we evolved from apes might expect to see several concrete manifestations of their theory as Homo Sapiens produce at regular intervals all sorts of offspring: perhaps a three-headed, six-legged, winged monster capable of doing the 100 metres in fewer than five seconds. Some of our offspring of extraordinary shapes and capabilities, probably out of desire to free themselves from the evil machinations of their egocentric, avaricious, wicked and morally degraded parent race the Homo Sapiens, might well fly over to Jupiter and live there, forever and ever happy.

Since things did not come about by accident, and contrary to the lies of those who believe we arrived here by chance, an Intelligent Designer, the King of Glory, was at work to form the human being, the climax of His creation. He put a mechanism in place to keep human beings in the form in which He created them—dare I say, in His image?—and so we will remain as long as He, the Creator, wills it. So, at the very moment, in the twinkle of an eye, when one sperm penetrates the egg and fuses with its nucleus, the heart of the egg cell containing twenty-three single chromosomes, a thick wall incapable of penetration by competing sperm forms around the fertilised egg to prevent other sperm from entering and disturbing the union.

Indeed, in the same twinkle of an eye when the egg and the sperm vow to remain together 'til death do them part, heaven instantaneously sanctions and seals the union.

Surely, when the egg and sperm declare to the whole world "'Till death do us part," they mean it to the letter. It is a union for life; it is not the kind sealed today and broken tomorrow; it is not a marriage showered with intense kissing before paparazzi cameras and the press, only to break up in curses and acrimony before the family court. Do you still want to assign chance to the mystery just described? You might as well dream of becoming a lotto millionaire, for it is easier for you to guess six numbers correctly out of forty-nine than for the miracle of conception to come about from mere chance.

We would imagine that always when the sperm of Father A meets the egg of Mother B they would produce offspring who look identical to each other. Imagine you came to my village, Mpintimpi, and requested to meet the children of Kofi Gyamfi and Amma Owusuah, and all five boys were one hundred percent identical. In the same way, you could not distinguish the three girls from one another.

The world could do with a few identical twins here and there, but for that to become a rule rather than the exception would lead to great confusion. I might have done something at school that warranted a reprimand; at that moment, Edmund, who though two years my senior was just about my size, could have appeared and claimed it was he, not me, who was the culprit.

Humankind, through disobedience to the Divine, has brought much confusion into the world. The Almighty God, however, is not a God of confusion, so in that regard he found a way out. To overcome the problem, the Divine ordained that during the sperm and egg production process, a random mixing of chromosome material should take place. As a result, the information used to produce each sibling of a particular parent is unique.

This random mixing of chromosome material occurs only during the production of sperm and eggs. I know proponents of chance evolution will come up with an explanation as to why this is the case. As for me, the poor village boy from rural Mpintimpi born into the most deprived conditions imaginable and raised by the Mighty Hands of the God of Hosts to make Mr. Something out of Mr. Nought, I will join King David to sing praises to the Rock of Ages, for I am wonderfully made.

Chapter 2
The Million-Dollar Baby

I will now highlight some of the wonders that take place from the time of our conception until the time of our birth. Someone has said that at the time of our birth we are already nine months old. This is indeed true, for from the moment when the genetic material of Mr. Sperm and Miss Egg join in their life-long union, an individual is present. Yes, at the precise moment a sperm joins an egg, the complex genetic blueprint for every detail of human development—sex, hair and eye colour, height, and skin tone—are already mapped out.

By approximately the fifth week of the union, the individual's heart has begun to beat. By the end of the fourth week, the spinal cord, muscles, and nerves have become apparent; we can see arms, legs, eyes, and ears. I will not delve into all the details regarding the stages of development in our mother's womb. It is better to leave that to the experts.

Before I proceed, I want us to pause for reflection. I am sure you have recently walked past a woman heavily pregnant with child, a woman expecting her baby in a few days. What were some of the thoughts that went through your mind? Did it include things like:

Why doesn't her stomach burst?

How is she able to breathe?

Where does she find the extra space for food and drink?

Maybe you take such matters for granted. If so, I urge you to spend a short while to ponder them.

Considering yourself may help in your deliberations. You may look back to the recent past when, extremely hungry, someone offered you rich and delicious food—steak, salmon, caviar, turkey— in abundant quantity and told to eat as much as you could.

The cells in your mouth having gone to work to produce an abundant flow of saliva in anticipation of the rich repast, you set about to fill your stomach with the tasty meal. It did not take long, though, before you felt the pressure in your belly; while you might have wished to consume more of the delectable meal, your stomach would not permit you.

I recall similar moments in my life. When I was a child growing up in the impoverished conditions of rural Ghana, once in a blue moon, especially at Christmas, my parents served what to us was a delicacy—a special version of our traditional meal *fufu*. On such special occasions, *fufu* was specially prepared with hard chicken boiled in groundnut soup and poured into a ball created by pounding boiled plantain and cassava together in a wooden mortar. I took advantage of the rare opportunity to fill my stomach to the brim. Soon, however, I began to feel the tension and my breathing became laboured. To my dismay, I realised there was a limit to my body's food reservoir.

If such is the case with the stomach lying in its usual position with no outside pressure, what would be the situation of a woman nearing her term, with a baby weighing about 3.5 kg lying in her womb? Fluid weighing another 2 kg surrounds the baby. The largely expanded womb and its contents exercise considerable pressure not only on the stomach itself, but also on the wall of the abdomen.

Moving a step further, we consider that in certain areas of our globe, my native Ghana included, some women, even when they are heavily pregnant, carry out strenuous work—carrying loads on their heads from their farms, bowing to harvest crops, manually washing clothes. One imagines that the atheist, contemplating the remarkable design and endurance of the human body, would come to recognise the hand of the Almighty God at work.

Is it not amazing what the womb is capable of achieving? The womb of a woman, known as the uterus, when not pregnant measures about eight centimetres in length, 5 cm in width and about 2.5 cm in thickness. The extent of expansion that this small mass of muscle undergoes in order to harbour the unborn child is simply incredible!

The self-acclaimed atheist sends out his sperm to impregnate his wife. While he jets from continent to continent to poison the minds of others with the story that there is no God, his offspring has the privilege of developing peacefully in the womb created by the King of Kings. What a big heart the Lord my Shepherd has!

Familiarity, it is said, breeds contempt. In this vein, we fail to appreciate the role the Creator has assigned to the womb unless something goes wrong. To remedy this, we should pay a visit to the intensive care unit of a neonatal and premature ward of a modern hospital to acquaint ourselves with the high-tech machines installed to help babies who for some reason have decided, prematurely, to leave the comfort of their mother's womb for the hazardous conditions on earth. For such babies, survival over the initial days and weeks of their lives on our planet is precarious.

After the staff have taken us through the unit and shown us the various machines and how they function, revealing to us the resources, energy, and time they invest to help the premature arrivals survive, we will begin, hopefully, to appreciate the wonders of God's creation.

Several years ago, when I was residing in Hanover, Germany, a little German child took the nickname of One-Million-Dollar Baby. This is how that child came to acquire that title:

The parents were holidaying in the U.S. when the highly pregnant visitor from Germany went into labour several weeks ahead of term. Eventually she delivered her baby in a hospital there. As might be expected, she was grateful to the hospital for the around-the-clock-care accorded to her premature child.

The shock soon came home to her, however. After her premature baby had spent a few weeks in the neonatal unit in the land of Uncle Sam, the hospital presented her with a bill near one million dollars! Imagine the consternation of parents if our Almighty Father demanded from them one million dollars for having utilised the womb He created to enable their offspring to develop.

Those familiar with the hectic pace of a neonatal intensive care unit and the stressful life of a premature baby in an incubator—barely arrived on earth and fighting organisms bent on destroying them— might compare this with the life of an unborn baby. Compare this to a child resting peacefully in Mama's comfortable womb at no extra cost to the health budget of his or her mother's country of residence, where they are unperturbed by the hurly burly outside world. When Mama feeds, baby feeds; when Mama breathes oxygen, the baby absorbs it from her bloodstream; when the baby grows tired or bored, he or she goes to sleep; when he or she feels like jumping about for a while, he or she does so in mother's womb. And why bother walking to the toilet to discard urine? He or she merely passes it into the surrounding fluid to be passed into mother's bloodstream for disposal.

If only those claiming there is no God would sit down to reflect. If only they would pause for a moment to consider how God preserved them in their mother's womb as they lay there, helpless. Oh man or woman of letters who has published repeatedly your ideas denying the existence of God, have you really given thought to your beginning— to the time when you lay helpless in your mother's womb? Do you know who preserved you when you lay there, helpless?

Oh, beautiful model jetting from continent to continent to capitalize on your beauty without any thought for your Maker! Oh, well-read Professor Dawkins, you who think you have gained so much insight into the physical world you have decided to deny the existence of your Creator, have you taken thought regarding how He preserved you in your mother's womb as you lay there, helpless?

Let us stay with the womb for a while longer.

As we noted earlier, the uterus of a non-pregnant woman is a small, muscular bag. After fertilization, the egg implants itself into the wall of the womb. Simultaneous to the development of the individual formed, the fertilized egg co-operates with the uterus to develop a sponge-like substance, the placenta, to serve as a medium for the exchange of substances between mother and the developing foetus.

Why the placenta develops at the time it does is a question I shall leave to atheists and adherents of chance evolution to answer. I imagine them coming up with an explanation along these lines: "That is part of the adaptation process in the matter of evolution. To adapt to life in water the fish developed gills; to adapt to life on land humans developed lungs; to adapt to fly in the air birds developed wings." So their academic dissertations would have us believe.

Adaptation! They tell us we walked on all fours, then we adapted, and now we walk on two legs. In the face of increasing energy prices and pollution, soon we will all develop wings that will enable us to fly from place to place without need for expensive fuel that only adds to the pollution of the environment.

Count me out, please, from those who attribute our existence to chance. No, I believe in a Creator who planned and executed everything with precision.

In the case of the fertilized egg, the order reaches it from Almighty God to implant itself on the walls of the womb, and so it happens! Mysteriously, both the fertilized egg and the wall of the womb cooperate to develop the placenta, which serves as a link between the mother and the developing baby, allowing for the exchange of substances between the loving mother and her child. Mother's blood passes nutrients, oxygen, hormones, and antibodies into the developing foetus. The foetus in turn passes on waste products to the blood of the pregnant mother for excretion.

I want to pause here to dwell briefly on another wonder of God's making. We know in the meantime that there are different blood types circulating in our veins. For our present discussion we shall settle with the four main blood groups, which we will call A, B, AB and O.

Ask anyone in the medical profession who has accidentally transfused, for example, blood group A into the veins of a person with blood group B, or the other way round, and that person will reveal the consequences of such a mishap. Such an unfortunate mix-up can, in the worst-case scenario, lead to the death of the individual involved.

Now, a mother in whose veins blood group A is flowing can give birth to a baby endowed with blood group B (depending on the blood of his/her father). The question one could ask is why mother and baby don't perish, given the proximity of their two distinct blood groups.

The answer is simple and amazing: the Divine considered the matter by making sure there is no direct mixture of the blood of the unborn child and the expectant mother.

Another marvel needs highlighting—namely, the principle of blood circulation in the unborn child vis-à-vis blood circulation after birth. I will return to the matter later when I reflect on the heart and blood circulation in general. For the moment, however, suffice it to know that immediately when we arrive on earth, when the doctor or midwife severs our umbilical cords from the placenta, a significant adjustment occurs in the process of circulation to meet the challenges of living a life independent of our connection to mother's circulatory system.

Before I leave this field, I will touch briefly on the matter of breathing. The unborn child resting comfortably in mother's womb does not breathe. Why is this? The answer confirms that Someone, rather than mere chance, brought us here.

The main function of breathing is the exchange of air. Since there is no air in the womb, there is also no need for breathing to take place. It would be a sheer waste of energy. The end goal of breathing is oxygenation of blood and the elimination of carbon dioxide. The placenta assumes this role during the period we are developing in our mother's womb.

Almighty God did not leave matters to chance, however. First, He caused the lungs of the unborn child to develop in anticipation of life on earth.

How would He trigger the breathing mechanism, dormant during our forty-week stay in the womb, into action? Our intelligent Creator assigned that role to an area in the lower part of the brain stem referred to as the medulla oblongata. Moments after our birth, a series of events in the heart and placenta contribute to a sharp fall in oxygen content of the blood flowing through our veins. The respiratory centre in our brain soon becomes aware of the life-threatening situation and immediately discharges alarm signals to trigger the breathing mechanism. How ordinary chance could have conceived such a smart plan is a question I would challenge the gurus of chance evolution to answer.

Chapter 3
The Arduous Journey to Planet Earth

T hus far, we have spent about forty weeks in our mother's womb and all of our organs have developed sufficiently to enable us to live an independent life under the conditions on earth. Here, another mechanism we can only describe as miraculous, namely labour, sets in.

It is yet another puzzling issue to figure out: how does the body know the seed it is carrying is ripe to be delivered?

We know that when the time comes for us to be born, hormones flow through the body and result in the contraction of the womb and the initiation of the labour process. The issue to consider is why in the overwhelming proportion of cases, labour sets in only when the unborn child has reached maturity. Why is it that in all expectant mothers, no matter where they reside, the period between conception and delivery is the same?

Why does nearly every child born into the world go through the standard movement through the birth canal?

These and countless other observations concerning the functioning of the human body confirm one important fact—that a Powerful and Intelligent Designer was behind our creation.

Now, dear reader, have you had the opportunity to witness at first hand the process of a normal childbirth?

In my opinion, all those who call themselves atheists, who spit on the face of God Almighty, who have made their names researching on the matter of evolution—yes, the fans of Charles Darwin, the hero of chance evolution—should have the opportunity to witness human birth. If they would not allow pride to blind their judgment, they would begin to reconsider their stance. It is indeed a solemn happening! We are not ordinary mammals that originated from mammalian-like reptiles, as some would have us believe; indeed, we are *something else*—in fact, we are the climax of God's creation.

Surely the events surrounding human birth, the tension, the excitement, the solemn atmosphere, bear witness to the fact that a more powerful being—not an ordinary mammal, not an ordinary being, but rather someone special, the climax of God's creation—is visiting the earth!

Even the journey of the unborn baby through the birth canal is, in itself, a miracle. Because of the anatomy of the birth canal, we cannot pass straight through it at birth. Instead, we have to make important positional changes as we travel. At several stages during our journey through the birth canal we have to, step by step, adjust our body here and there until our eyes see the light of day!

To get a good picture of how we master our journey through the birth canal, we might think of a time when we tried to move furniture or other items into our home and realised the items concerned were too big to pass through our doors, so we began to think and plan. Soon it occurred to us that though we could not get the items straight through the doors, we could achieve our goal if we did some turning and adjusting of the items as we moved. We set out to work. At certain stages, we turned the items through certain angles; at certain stages, we even had to carry the items upside down. Yet with some manoeuvring, we succeeded in carrying the objects through the doors. This is exactly what happens to an unborn child on his or her journey to the world.

The question I wish to put to those who say we originated by accident from single cells several million years ago is simple. From where does a baby journeying through the narrow birth canal get its instructions to do the turns and bends needed for delivery?

As we noted earlier, after fertilization the womb and foetus co-operate to develop the placenta. Throughout our nine-month stay in the womb, the placenta remains firmly attached to the walls of the uterus. The moment we leave the womb and arrive on earth, something miraculous begins to happen. Suddenly, as if acting on a command to "get rid of it," the walls of the womb begin to discard the placenta.

We may liken the matter to a situation in which one rents a room or an apartment for a period. When the time comes for one to leave, one forgets some items in the room. The owner of the property comes to inspect the room and is not amused to find those items. Since the tenancy agreement has expired, the property owner employs the right to discard the items on the street. In the same way, the walls of the uterus simply discard the placenta after its main occupant has left.

Instead of believing the lie the atheists and their compatriots who hold onto the theory of chance evolution are spreading, I urge you to contemplate your navel. Your navel is, in effect, the remains of your umbilical cord. Every day when you look at it, be grateful to Him who took care of you while you lay helpless in your mother's womb.

Chapter 4
Delicious Mother's Milk Sustaining Us

A
s I browsed the Internet one day, I came across the website of a high school in the U.S. Visitors were welcome to join them in their various classes to gain insight into what teachers taught there. Eventually, I ended up in the science class of students of the upper grade; I joined the class for a lesson on mammals.

Among the first things I learned was that mammals evolved from flesh-eating reptiles called Cynodonts about 190 million years ago. The figure 190 million years stunned me! "How did the experts arrive at the figure?" I wondered. I decided not to give up early, but to stay with the class until the end.

The lesson went on to list the main characteristics of mammals:

1) Animals with vertebrae or backbone
2) Warm-blooded animals; that is, they have a warm internal body temperature which is independent of the temperature of their surroundings
3) Animals with hair
4) Animals that deliver their babies alive (the young from only three species of mammals are said to hatch from eggs)

5) Drink milk from the mammary glands of their mothers from birth until they can eat solid food

For the sake of our present discussion, I shall concentrate on the fifth point, namely that a mammal is an animal that drinks milk from its mother's mammary glands when it is born until it can eat solid food on its own.

The human baby referred to earlier, having successfully completed the strenuous journey through the birth canal, now experiences the first hunger pangs. In reaction to this, our new arrival screams and yells at the top of his or her voice, looking for a means to still thirst and hunger.

Before I proceed on the matter, allow me to return to the science class. Remember that the children in the school I visited are in effect being thought that we—mammals by classification—evolved from Cynodonts.

I decided therefore to take a closer look at my supposed ancestors, Mr. and Mrs. Cynodont. As stated, scientists suppose they lived on the earth several million years ago and possessed skin, yet lacked scales and fur—being, it is alleged, a kind of naked lizard. Experts say they are not sure whether Mrs. Cynodont possessed breasts that provided milk for her offspring.

The only evidence the experts say led them to associate Cynodonts with mammals were in fossil finds. The honorable men and women in the field of Palaeontology want us to believe we evolved from Cynodonts.

This brings me back to the helpless human baby we left earlier, screaming even louder, demanding someone provide him or her the breast milk he or she so urgently requires. Now, as we learned from the high school science lesson, young mammals, like the human baby above, need milk to survive in the early stages of their lives.

My question for those who want us to believe that mammals evolved from reptiles is how did the first young mammal, after it had evolved from the Cynodonts, reptiles that by definition do not possess mammary glands or breasts to produce milk, survive during the first several days of its life?

Indeed, who fed milk to the first baby mammal after it evolved from the Cynodont?

Or, did the first mammals evolve as adult entities from Cynodonts? We might as well picture Mr. and Mrs. Cynodont retiring to bed one night, only to awaken the next morning transformed into mammals!

Next question: did the mammals evolve consecutively or sequentially from the reptile-like beings? Was it today the mouse, tomorrow the cat, the next day the elephant? Or did the first mammal that evolved from the Cynodonts—let's assume they were Mr. and Mrs. Mouse—give birth over the course of time to the other remaining mammals?

We could presume Mr. and Mrs. Cat to be the first generation ancestors of Mr. and Mrs. Mouse; Mr. and Mrs. Antelope follow in the second generation (assuming the cats give their parents the chance to live on) and on, and on, and on it would go, the mouse producing all the mammals of the earth—human beings included.

I shall now return to the newborn baby who has just arrived on earth. The child, who one day will be champion of atheism, is only a few minutes old. Completely helpless and still suffering from hunger pangs, the baby screams loudly. The child would surely perish in a matter of days without life sustaining breast milk.

Almighty God, who unlike the proponents of chance evolution does not leave anything to chance, made provision to avert such a scenario long ago as He sat to contemplate His creation. He who says thing A, then goes on to say B and then C, right to the logical end, did not leave the survival of the newborn mammal to chance, but instead created the mammary glands, the breasts, to produce milk and feed young ones during the initial stages of their lives on earth.

Another aspect of breast-feeding in mammals in general and humans in particular worthy of pondering is this: Why do the breasts of the expectant mother suddenly begin to produce milk? Why don't those of non-pregnant mothers of the same age do the same?

In response, someone will tell me certain hormones produced by the body of the new mother cause lactation. But does that explain why? When we are driving our vehicle and danger crosses our path, is not our first thought or instinct to depress the brake pedal? Did the device, the brake pedal, arrive there by chance? Didn't the engineers of BMW, Ford, Mercedes, and Toyota sit down and think things out? "How do we get a vehicle of considerable mass and equipped with considerable horse power to come to a halt once it has been set in motion?" they might have asked each other. After spending several hours pondering over the matter, they came up with the braking system.

Imagine that we parked such a vehicle somewhere and an alien from beyond our planet—although I do believe life is found only on our planet—arrived and began to take a critical look at the automobile, into the minute detail regarding the principles at work in it, and suddenly was inspired to speak about its accidental origin. It would be an insult to the ingenuity of the automobile industry's learned engineers and the artisans who spent hours on end designing the vehicle. There is yet another issue we usually take for granted: who taught us, when we arrived on earth, how to suck milk? This is surely something beyond the understanding of ordinary mortals. Unfortunately, my mother is no longer alive, so I am unable to consult her to find out the manner in which I went about the business of sucking—did I do it gently or in a wild manner? If you are among those blessed to have a living mother, you may approach her to find out about the matter.

Though we might have differed in style, it boils down in the end to the same thing—shortly after our arrival, the midwife or nurse placed us near mamma's breast and we soon began to suck on the nipple. The question worthy of asking is how did we know then that the sucking action would reward us with a flow of breast milk? Further, the breasts of the new mother do not usually run out, no matter how much energy the newborn baby invests into sucking them empty. Indeed, the more the infant sucks them, the more milk they produce. On the other hand, if for some reason the new mother does not breastfeed, the breast stops producing milk within days.

I recognize in this matter another intelligent mechanism the Divine Designer put into place to ensure the newborn baby's demand for breast milk is satisfied, as long as the need exists, and to make certain that when such a demand no longer exits, the breast will cease producing. Who are you, ordinary human flesh, to question the wisdom of the Lord my Shepherd? We are indeed wonderfully made, friends!

Come and join me, all who inhabit the earth, to give Almighty God some well-deserved applause. Indeed, the Big Boss of creation does indeed deserve praise and worship.

Chapter 5
From the Cradle to Our First Steps

Another circumstance that throws the concept of chance evolution completely into disarray is the issue of child development.

According to theory, all life developed from a primordial cell. I want to repeat the question I asked earlier—did the first mammal evolve as a baby or an adult?

If it were a baby, we are justified in wondering who took care of the baby human being as it lay helpless, crying. Who put the child to bed? Who changed the nappies (of course at that time there were no nappies, but I use the term to bring the matter home to modern man)? Indeed, who tidied and cleaned the first human baby that evolved from another organism?

Or, do the proponents of evolution want to tell us we evolved as adults, like a monkey changing in the twinkle of an eye into an adult human being?

The Bible says Almighty God created Adam and Eve. He created them as adults, for the Almighty God was able to communicate with them. Adam, though one day old, probably looked like a twenty or thirty year old.

In the same way, Almighty God created the whole of the animal population as adults; in the case of ordinary animals, He just called them into existence. Those who say they cannot believe in God Almighty simply have no idea of the dimensions we talk about when we consider His powers—immense, immense, immense! His power, rightly so, is beyond anything our mental faculties, limited as they are, can fathom. It is a fact that at the time of creation, no human being was around. Even Adam and Eve came upon the scene later.

We ask ourselves whether it is such a big deal for the Power behind the universe to reveal unto His servant Moses the facts of creation in the form of a film (Who said it was we human beings that discovered the technology behind the film?). The Almighty long ago laid down all of the inventions we boast of, or the technology behind them. It was up to us to go around cracking, cracking, and cracking our brains to discover them. Sometimes Almighty God flashed the insight needed to develop an engine, a drug, or a technology into the human mind. Suddenly, a concept our intellect could not see came forward for the benefit of humankind.

If the world continues as it is, and we have the privilege of revisiting it one hundred years from now, we shall be amazed at what our offspring might have in the meantime been able to conceive. We might be full of wonder about it, but as far as God Almighty is concerned, these things are today even in existence, for, indeed, the Most High God knows the beginning from the end and the end from the beginning.

Those who His Spirit has not touched one way or the other may consider what they have just read to be absurd. It is not so for the author of these lines. Oh yes, I do know I am serving a living God—who, in His sheer grace towards me, once revealed to me in a dream what was to happen in my life at a later date. His did not fulfil His promise to me the next day, or the following year. Indeed, it took three good years. Yet the promise was fulfilled, though not without struggles, disappointment, and apparent failure. Yes, Almighty God had spoken, and nothing in the world, Satan and his horde of soldiers included, could hinder the fulfilment of the prophecy. (For more details, please refer to my autobiography *The Call that Changed My Life*.) As far as I am concerned, therefore, it is comprehensible that The Living Power behind all that is seen and unseen, the Divine Shepherd of my soul, should have revealed His creation to Moses and at the same time empowered him to put the gist of whatever he saw on paper.

I shall now move on to give a brief overview of how the newborn baby develops during the first twelve months of existence on earth.

It is incredible, the realization that a helpless newborn child on the labor ward somewhere in the world could one day become the President of the U.S.A., the Secretary General of the United Nations, or a great scientist who would make astounding discoveries. Yet, no one around that particular child would be aware of the fact. We could indeed spend volumes upon volumes philosophizing on the human miracle.

I have personally had the privilege to watch our three children grow from day one to their present ages of fifteen, eleven, and seven years respectively. Child development is a miracle beyond belief. A textbook may give us a theoretical picture, but I think practical experience goes well beyond all that a textbook can narrate. Although our fifteen-year-old girl creates the impression of knowing better than her father—whose grey hairs are gradually winning the race to replace the few black ones left on his head, and whose brain cells fight hard to overcome memory loss and keep pace with a fast-changing world—she was, fifteen years ago, completely helpless and entirely dependent on her parents to help her find her way in life. Contrary to what the proponents of chance evolution want to imply, if we had left her alone to struggle to survive, she would with certainty not have survived but rather returned to Almighty God who placed His life in her.

Her parents, particularly her mother, played with bravado the role entrusted them by Almighty God, to raise her up until such time that she would be able to live an independent life. That she has come so far in life is a feat we as parents do not wish to ascribe to our doing, but to the miraculous hands of her Creator and ours.

Here I shall provide a brief overview of how a newborn child develops during the first twelve months of life on earth. We usually double our birth weight after six months, and triple it between nine and twelve months. During this period, we develop the ability to learn and remember. We begin to recognize and interact with loved ones and start to understand that people and objects still exist even when they are out of sight.

We also undergo emotional and social development. In the first month, we express emotion mainly by crying and grimacing or displaying an alert and bright face. In a loving environment, we form a bond with our parents. By the time we are about four months of age, we learn to smile, coo, and move our arms when we become excited.

By the age of five months, we show a clear preference for a loved one. In the following months, we display "separation protest" and "stranger anxiety" as ways of demonstrating a growing attachment to the person with whom we have bonded. Such a bond provides a foundation for future relationships, teaching us to love and to trust others.

After birth, our movements begin to become more controlled and deliberate as the reflexes we possessed as newborn babies fade. By six months, we are coordinated enough to suck our toes and strong enough to sit with light support. By the time we have been here for about ten months, many of us can stand with some support.

I shall pause for a moment to reflect on the matter of language development. It is no secret babies are open to learning and quickly absorb the language around them. This happens quite independently of the original language spoken by the parents. A child born, for example, to Swedish parents, who we take from them at the time of birth and place in the care of a Hausa-speaking couple in Northern Nigeria will eventually pick up the Hausa language and speak it as if it were the language of the child's biological parents. In the same way, if we hand over a child born to Jewish parents to Arabic-speaking parents, the child will pick up the Arabic language; this takes me back to the Bible. In it, we read that at the beginning we all spoke the same language and that different tongues came later when out of pride humanity attempted to put up the tower of Babel.

The ability of a newborn baby to pick up language, while not constituting absolute proof, gives credence to the fact that at the beginning humankind spoke one language. The Bible underlines the reason for the present state of affairs.

Chapter 6
The Brain Seeking to Understand
Its Own Actions

A lmighty Father, after He had created the universe and all things seen and unseen, including the fishes of the sea, the birds of the air, and the beasts of the land, decided to create human beings in His own image to act as caretakers of His beautiful creation.

I feel Almighty God had two options to consider before creating humans. Either He could create humans as robots that He would continuously remote control from heaven (imagine having to seek permission from heaven before going to empty our bowels or pass water!) or make us independent of His direct, around-the-clock control. In the end, the Master of creation decided on the latter.

How was He to empower us with the ability to go about our activities ourselves? In this case, again, I recognize two options at His disposal: either set up a single command centre in the body to coordinate all activities of the individual, or set up command centres at different spots in the body, each imbued with the responsibility of control over specific bodily organs.

In the end, Almighty God came up with a solution involving a single command centre. This leads me to the brain, the command centre of the body.

The human brain is profoundly mysterious. There is no rational relationship between the soft, jelly-like matter making up the brain and its function; what association can we draw between the jelly-like tissue and the airplane or the spaceship it is capable of designing? Though today we are in a position to understand some of its functions, the most brilliant neurosurgeon or neurologist will confess, if honest, to not fully understanding all of the intricate ins and outs of the functioning of the brain.

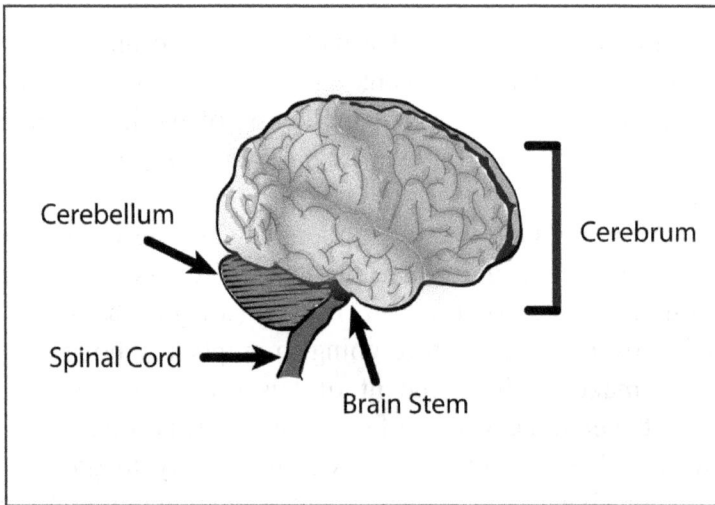

Fig. 4. The brain can be divided into four parts: the cerebrum, the diencephalon, the brain stem and the cerebellum.

Weighing about 1.5 kilogram on the average, the human brain is made up of around 100 billion cells. We would expect an intelligent designer to place a delicate structure made of tissue that even the slightest jolt could injure, and which is capable of profound functions, in a protective cage—which is indeed the case. Three tough membranes called meninges surround it to offer the needed protection. The space between the brain and the meninges contains a clear fluid, which cushions it, provides it with energy, and protects it against infection. Most importantly, however, a bony shell, the skull, encases the brain to protect it from injury.

Because it is so complex, I will not go into great detail trying to explain how it functions. I will only provide an overview.

We can divide the brain into four parts: the cerebrum, the diencephalon, the brain stem, and the cerebellum.

Cerebrum

The cerebrum is the largest part of the brain. It sits on top of the brain, rather like a mushroom cap covering its stalk. It has a heavily folded grey surface. The front section of the cerebrum, known as the frontal lobe, is responsible for speech, thought, emotion, and skilled movements.

Behind this is the parietal lobe, which perceives and interprets sensations like touch, temperature, and pain.

Behind this, at the centre and back of your cerebrum, is a region called the occipital lobe, which detects and interprets visual images. On either side of the cerebrum are the temporal lobes, which are involved in hearing and storing memory. The cerebrum splits down the middle into two halves called hemispheres that communicate with each other.

Cerebellum

The cerebellum is the second largest part of the brain. It sits underneath the back of the cerebrum. It is involved in coordinating muscles to allow precise movements and control of balance and posture.

The diencephalon sits beneath the middle of the cerebrum and on top of the brain stem. It contains two important structures called the thalamus and the hypothalamus. The thalamus acts as a relay station for incoming sensory nerve impulses, sending them on to appropriate regions of the brain for processing. The hypothalamus plays a vital role in keeping conditions inside the body constant. It does this by regulating body temperature, thirst, and hunger, amongst other things, such as controlling the release of hormones from the nearby pituitary gland. The hormones from the pituitary gland play an important role in the menstrual cycle, for example.

The brain stem is responsible for regulating many life support mechanisms, such as heart rate, blood pressure, digestion and breathing. It also regulates the wake-and-sleep cycle.

It is true that lower animals such as gorillas, chimpanzees, and dogs also possess brains boasting a similar consistency to that of humans; in the case of the climax of His creation, He decided to endow our brain with extraordinary capabilities so intricate it borders on the mysterious.

Sometimes I ask myself why, aware of the potential risk in endowing the human mind with such extraordinary intelligence, did Almighty God place such terrific intelligence at our disposal.

The lion is mighty and ferocious. Place a human being before him, and he will tear the luckless human apart. The elephant is massive and terribly heavy. Should he trample on you and me, our intestines would probably gush out of our bodies. Expose us to the crocodile and he will devour us in no time. While we cannot match the beasts in physical power, they are no match for us on the level of brainpower: we have sent some of our race to the moon, an achievement the beasts of the earth have little hope of achieving. Yes, Almighty God endowed humanity with great intelligence to enable us take dominion over His creation. Or did our Almighty God not reckon initially with the fall of man when He put such vast capabilities at our disposal? (The same way mortal man confides precious secrets in a beloved one, unknowing that a few months later the relationship will go sour, leading to our confidant betraying us before the world.) Of course, I do believe that Almighty God, who knows the beginning from the end and vice-versa, was aware of the risk involved in creating humanity in His image and imbuing us with profound intelligence. Since His thoughts are not our thoughts, neither are His ways our ways. I can only speculate as to why He chose to take the path He took.

In any case, He gave us enormous mental capability. Then came the fall, and suddenly the same human brain that in time would create the civilian jumbo jet to facilitate movement of people around the world would also invent the B-52 bomber to create havoc. The same brain structure that came up with the Web to facilitate global communication was the same brain that infiltrated the Internet with pornography—even that involving children. The same brain flooded the Web with instructions on making bombs and carrying out terrorist activities.

As another example, the human brain, having come to understand the principles behind the menstrual cycle, sought not only to breach the copyright laws of the Almighty by producing synthetic forms of some of the hormones that regulate the cycle, but also to manipulate it to suit our whims and caprices. A woman approached me the other day to request medication to help her postpone her menstrual cycle; she was leaving for holiday and did not want to be inconvenienced!

This is not the forum in which to discuss the pros and cons of the contraceptive pill, but when you hear people use phrases like, "The introduction of the pill has led to the sexual revolution," you get a picture of what that person is driving at. It is as if those who lived prior to the introduction of the pill lived in bondage and required a revolution to set them free.

The superiority of the human brain vis-à-vis those of ordinary animals is reflected in the large size of the human brain as a ratio to the body. In humans, this is about 1.8 percent, whereas in gorillas the brain makes up only 0.333 percent of its body weight.

That part of our body that distinguishes humanity from any other creature on earth is a miracle beyond measure. That such an intricate organ could have developed by accident is a matter that stretches my understanding to the utmost, to put it mildly.

Chapter 7
The Fabulous Electric Transmitter

T he spinal cord, which one might describe as an elongation of the brain, runs from the neck to the hip area. It transmits nerve messages between the brain and the rest of the body. As a way of highlighting the relationship between the brain and the spinal cord, I shall narrate the experience I had as I sat down to write this chapter.

As I took my position before my computer to write this portion, I switched on the electric lamp to provide light. It would not shine. "What is wrong?" I wondered. Soon I realised I had not switched on the socket on the mains.

We can draw a parallel between the lamp and the electric mains with the relationship between the spinal cord and brain. The spinal cord is a kind of electric cable joined to the brain to transmit impulses from the brain to the rest of the body. It performs its function by means of nerves that branch from it to transmit signals to the rest of the body, for example our hands and legs. Thus, when the brain wants the body to pick up an object, it sends an impulse through the spinal cord. The nerves pick up the waves from the spinal chord and transmit the impulse to the hands.

My brain and spinal cord, together with the nerves supplying my hands, have been busy throughout the time I have been writing.

The ideas come by inspiration from the Divine Designer. My brain transmits impulses through the spinal cord to my hands that go about tapping on the computer's keyboard before me.

I was personally humbled when I first had the opportunity to view the spinal cord with my naked eye. It was during my first-year anatomy class at the Hanover Medical School in Northern Germany. I opened my mouth in awe and began to ask myself how a tiny, cord-like structure could perform the function with which it is associated.

I have mentioned in several instances in this book that we normally take things for granted in life until something goes terribly wrong. That takes me to the Twi proverb that translates into English approximately as follows: "It is in the absence of his wife that a husband comes to realise her worth."

Let us consider the case of the young, able woman who yesterday had been going about life normally, with big plans for the future. Then something goes terribly wrong—a tragic accident results in the spinal cord being severed at a particular point in its course. This interrupts all communication from the brain with the area of the body below the damage. When she wants to move her hands, she cannot; she wants to move her legs but cannot. Think about it—damage to the tiny cord, several times narrower than that of her little finger, at the level of her waist and she is no longer capable of lifting her limbs. More embarrassing, she wants to control her urine but cannot.

For a while, our scientists have been at work to find a way whereby they can repair a damaged spinal cord and help it resume its function. I can only wish them all the best in their endeavours. I can only wish and pray that if they one day succeed, they will give praise and honour where it is due, to Him who created that marvel, that they will learn to acknowledge the Person whose ingenuity brought about that mysterious structure in the first place.

Let us learn to give praise where praise is due, friends. Join me in giving glory to our Creator. As I said elsewhere, we may not understand His workings; we may be baffled as to why there is so much suffering in the face of such a powerful God. That should not, however, let us lose sight of one thing, friends—that all of this could not have come about by accident.

Chapter 8
River of Life

I want to reiterate the fact that I am one hundred percent convinced an Intelligent Designer is at work in our bodies. He created and placed us on earth for a purpose. During our stay here, we need energy to survive. We also have to grow. Finally, we need to defend ourselves from infectious organisms. To facilitate the supply of nutrients to the cells of the body and the elimination of waste products that build up because of cellular activity, Almighty God came up with blood, which, without exaggeration, we can refer to as the river of life.

Blood has two components: the liquid, plasma, and the cells floating in it. Dissolved in the plasma are various substances including electrolytes, nutrients, vitamins, hormones, clotting factors, and infection-fighting antibodies. The cellular part of blood is about ninety-nine percent red blood cells; the remaining one percent is white blood cells.

The main function of blood is to transport oxygen and nutrients to the cells of the body. It also transports waste products of metabolism to organs such as the kidney and liver for excretion from the body. The adult human body contains approximately five litres of blood; it makes up seven to eight percent of a person's body weight.

As I mentioned in an earlier chapter, there are four major blood types: A, B, AB, and O. The blood types are determined by proteins called antigens found on the surfaces of the red blood cells. There are two types of these, called antigen A and B respectively. The person with blood group A has antigen A on the surface of the red blood cells, whereas the person with blood group B has antigen B. There are instances when both antigens are present. We say such a person has blood group AB. Finally, a person whose cells are devoid of either antigen has blood group O.

Blood performs the following functions: Cells continuously add waste products, secretions, and metabolites to blood while taking from it vital nutrients, oxygen, hormones, and other substances. Blood transports oxygen from the lungs to body tissues and transports the waste products of cellular metabolism and nutrients, hormones and enzymes. Blood also regulates clotting, body temperature, acid-base balance and protects us against harmful organisms through white cells and antibodies.

Blood is our lifeline. When we lose a considerable amount of it, the heart can no longer pump it effectively to the brain, and that leads to death.

Chapter 9
Clotting Factors

In the 27 April 2007 edition of the *GP*, a weekly medical journal in the UK, a doctor wrote with regard to the circulation of blood, "One of nature's remarkable achievements is how blood stays liquid inside the blood vessel and goes lumpy outside of the vessels."

As I just mentioned, Almighty God put blood, the river of life, into our vessels to facilitate the transport of nutrients. Each of us carries about five litres of the precious fluid. The loss of a considerable amount of it leads to death.

Having assigned blood such an important role in our existence, Almighty God considered how to avert losses, which eventually could lead to our deaths. This was essential, particularly from the point of view of the woman who has to undergo menstruation and childbirth.

He was also aware that during our stay here we would be subject to injuries. To avert a situation of that nature, Almighty God put a mechanism in place in our bodies that would lead to the clotting of blood the moment a vessel sustained damage. After the fall of man, the ability of blood to clot became even more important for our existence. Having rebelled against our Creator, humanity soon gave way to selfishness and greed, and men and women began to vent their frustration and anger against one another. Soon they began to fight each other. This took various forms, through the direct exchange of blows or indirectly, by way of weapons.

God also condemned humanity to till the land, which could lead to injuries that in turn could threaten to drain the body of its vital blood supply.

As the medical expert quoted above rightly put it, it is a wonder blood remains liquid within the vessels so long as the vessels have not suffered damage. The moment, however, the walls of the vessel are broken, a sophisticated clotting mechanism begins to avert bleeding and possible death.

I side with the medical expert that clotting is a wonder. What I do not agree with is the fact that she gives nature credit for the miracle. That is the way atheists, so-called naturalists, and all who refuse to credit Almighty God for our existence, seek to explain away such incredible phenomena we can assign only to Him in their desire to ease their conscience. So long as we assign such wonders to nature (others refer to Mother Nature), no one will hold them to account. On the other hand, they know that the moment they give Almighty God the credit, they will have to deal with the issue of commitment to His authority; if you accept the existence of the Big Boss of creation, why are you refusing to submit to Him? Thus, many use nature or Mother Nature as a smokescreen, or a means of sidestepping the issue of commitment and conscience. It is a convenient excuse not to accept the obvious, the convincing reality of God's existence.

The mechanism of blood clotting, to put it mildly, is a wonder of incredible proportions. How, indeed, could we survive on earth without the ability of our blood to clot? I, for one, would have bid farewell to planet earth a long time ago. Oh, how many times I injured myself as I helped my parents on our farms. Injury came by way of the cutlass we used to weed on the cocoa farms, or as we walked barefoot through the village, when the great toe could hit an object like a sharp stone.

Without clotting, the branch of medicine called surgery would never have been born, for the smallest surgical wound would have resulted in the patient's death. You may be able to think of countless other examples.

The principle behind the clotting of blood is so complicated it is enough to blow even the minds of the experts. Since I mean my discourse for the expert in the field of medicine as well as the non-professional, I do not consider it appropriate to delve into the details. I must confess it is a topic I tackled reluctantly. In the end, I adopted the strategy that bordered on what we generally know as "chew, pour, pass, and forget," whereby a student or pupil learns a topic well enough to pass an exam and forgets about it when the examination is over. Of course, I do read over the topic regularly in order not to forget it completely, but it still remains, for me, one of the more challenging topics of medicine.

This in essence is how the clotting mechanism works: as soon as a blood vessel is broken, the damaged wall responds to the injury by contraction. In other words, it pulls together automatically in an attempt to close the gap. Think about it—the Divine Designer put intelligence even into the walls of a blood vessel in order to deliver us from danger. Soon the alarm bell reaches several factors swimming in the blood. Like fire fighters on reserve duty, the body calls these factors into action only when danger knocks and they rush to the scene of the fire.

A mechanism then takes place to cause certain components of the blood, the platelets that gather at the site of the injury, to become sticky and clump together. In the course of time, they form a mass that stops the flow of blood. After the blood vessel heals, the clots dissolve back into the blood.

What is fascinating about the matter of blood clotting is that there are several factors involved in the process. Each of the factors must play the role assigned to it meticulously for the whole process to function properly. Like fire fighters who arrive at the scene of a fire to attempt to extinguish it, the several factors floating in our blood that bring about the clotting of blood must work as a team to ensure the clotting takes place.

There are instances when, in some individuals, some of the factors are either absent or not working effectively, as in the case of the disorder haemophilia. In this disorder, one factor is missing, and as a result the clotting process cannot function and the victim is in danger of bleeding to death.

How can complex substances appear at the right time in the right proportions and mix properly to clot blood and prevent death? I refuse to assign such a sophisticated mechanism to chance, nature, or Mother Nature. No, I believe with all my heart that God Almighty brought everything into existence. It was through His Divine Order, not by chance of evolution that it is so. It was so yesterday, it is so today, and it shall be so until the end of time.

Chapter 10
The Pump of Life

W hat value will liquid designed to serve as a lifeline to supply the body's cells and tissues with nutrients and oxygen have without a pump to circulate it around the body?

Since the universe and all it contains did not develop by chance but rather by design, the Designer considered this fact in coming up with a pump to take up that role.

The human heart: It is indeed another masterpiece of God's creation. It begins its pumping activity early in an individual's development and works dutifully around the clock. It works during the day, as we go about life's activities, and at night when we are deep asleep; it works in our joys and in our sorrows; it works in toil and in ease; it works in the cold of the winter and the heat of summer. Indeed, no matter the time of day, the season of the year, or the state of our minds, the automatic pump Almighty God fixed into our chests keeps dutifully pumping day in and day out to sustain us.

Assuming an average pumping rate of seventy per minute, our heart pumps 100,800 times a day, or 36,792,000 times a year. In a life spanning seventy years, that amounts to approximately 2.3 billion times. I have not even taken into consideration the number of pumps this hollow muscular organ undergoes during the time we rest in the wombs of our mothers. Indeed, the heart starts pumping around five weeks after our conception.

It is not my intention to provide a detailed description of how the heart is constructed. Those interested in the detail may consult relevant literature. The heart consists of two upper and two lower chambers. Each chamber in turn has two sections, making four compartments. Blood from the body, rich in carbon dioxide resulting from the reactions taking place in the cells, drains into the right upper chamber. From there it pumps into the right lower chamber, which in turn pumps it into the lungs. In the lungs, blood picks up oxygen and releases carbon dioxide. The oxygen-enriched blood drains into the left upper chamber, which pumps it into the left chamber. The left chamber then pumps it into the general circulation to complete the cycle.

Although the heart is a single organ, it acts as a double pump. The first pump carries oxygen-poor blood to the lungs and delivers oxygen-rich blood back to your heart. The second pump delivers oxygen-rich blood to every part of the body. In one day, your heart transports all your blood around your body about 1000 times! The description I have just given is true for the individual after birth. Before I proceed in my deliberations, I shall for a moment return to the unborn child, to consider the principle on which the circulation of blood centres in the child's case.

It is important to gain an understanding in comparing the two situations to appreciate the incredible intelligence Almighty God put into place in His creation. I hope the realization of this will lead us to appreciate the might of the God we serve. Throw fears to the dogs, dear brother! Throw fears to the dogs, dear sister! For indeed, we serve, without exaggeration, a really awesome God.

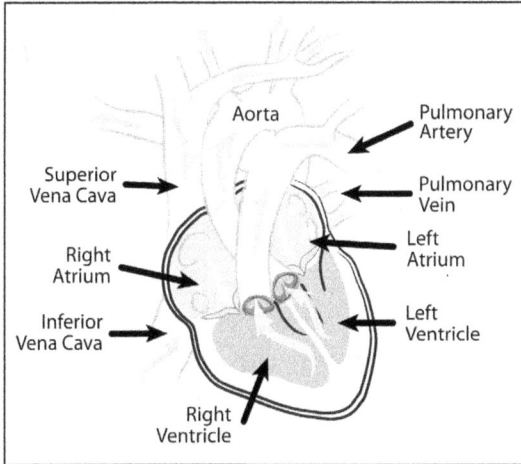

Fig. 5. The heart with arrows pointing to the direction of blood flow after birth. Basically, the heart comprises two upper and two lower chambers. Each chamber in turn is divided into two, making a total of four compartments.

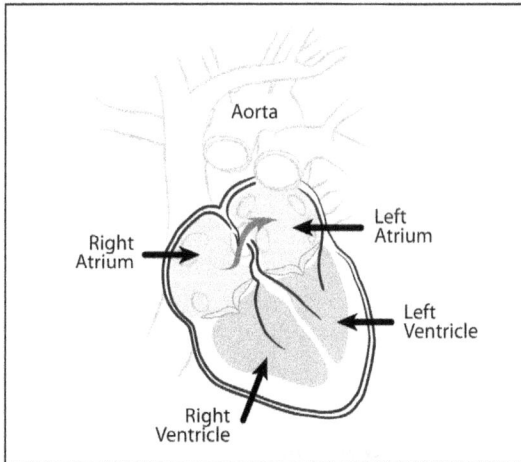

Fig. 6. In our mother's womb, purified blood coming from the mother enters the right upper chamber of the heart. The left and right upper chambers of the heart at this stage are connected by way of an opening called the foramen ovale.

When we are in our mother's womb the purified blood coming from the mother enters the right upper chamber of the heart. The left and right upper chambers of the heart at this stage connect by way of an opening. Most of the blood moves straight from the right upper chamber through the opening into the left upper chamber. It then travels from the left upper chamber into the left lower chamber. From there it flows into all parts of the body. The lungs at this stage play no role in the supply of oxygen to the foetus.

The moment we arrive on planet earth, however, the opening between the two upper chambers closes. Blood that reaches the heart from the right upper chamber, consequently, cannot travel directly into the left upper chamber, as was once the case. Instead, it pumps down into the right lower chamber. The right lower chamber now pumps the blood into the lungs. As stated above, the blood picks up oxygen and disposes of carbon dioxide upon reaching the lungs. It then travels from the lungs into the left upper chamber of the heart, then into the left chamber to continue on to various parts of the body.

We note in summary that in the foetus, oxygenated blood reached the right side of the heart from the placenta. At delivery, the course reverses. From now onward, blood depleted of oxygen and gathering from all parts of the body will flow into the right upper chamber to circulate into the right lower chamber. Oxygenated blood reaches the left side of the heart from the lungs. I wish to ask those who believe in chance evolution what caused this to happen. Was it chance? There is nothing like chance in the economy of God's creation. He planned and executed everything to a logical conclusion.

We can identify another piece of ingenuity concerning the construction of the heart. Our heart needs to pump blood continuously. Any pause in its activity, lasting even a few seconds, could be life threatening. We know from experience that the muscles of the legs and arms, what we call the skeletal muscles, have a tendency to become tired. Anyone who has walked a long distance or taken part in strenuous sporting activities will bear me out. Soon our muscles begin to hurt or cramp, causing out legs to want to "give in."

God Almighty decided, therefore, to use a special kind of muscle, a type of muscle that would never grow tired, to form our hearts.

Skeletal muscle cells require nerve impulse stimulation from the brain to contract. For example, when I want to type a key on my computer, my brain sends an electric signal through the spinal cord to the nerves branching from it. The nerves in turn cause the muscles controlling my fingers to contract not in an ordinary manner, but in a coordinated manner to enable me to execute exactly what I intend to do.

The responsibility of the heart is to pump blood around the clock, even when we are asleep and the conscious part of our brain is at rest. You may wonder how the heart can keep on pumping when we are sleeping. The Lord of the universe got around the problem by using special muscles to construct the heart. Indeed, these special muscles, known as cardiac muscles, are the only muscles of their kind in our body. Not only is the word "tired" unheard of in the world of the cardiac muscles, they are also able to contract on their own accord.

This is yet another miracle among the millions at work in our body!

The Creator, realizing that, left on their own, the spontaneous contractions of the heart muscles would remain uncoordinated, and result in the heart's pumping actions becoming ineffective, averted the situation by fixing into the right upper chamber a group of specialised cardiac muscles known as the sinoatrial node to assume the role of pace-maker and coordinate the rate of heartbeat.

Is there any challenger to Divine wisdom around? If so, take thought of the pump in your chest—the dutiful muscular pump pumping blood to nourish your brain even at the moment you are considering your arguments against Almighty God!

The Great Designer took further steps to ensure the pumping effectiveness of the heart by building a system of valves into the circulatory system to facilitate the flow of blood in a forward direction. This would not only facilitate blood flow, but also avert undue strain to the heart that might result in the regurgitation or backflow of blood. The valves within the heart itself and the vessels transporting blood to and from it ensure a forward flow of blood within the closed circulatory system.

The Great Designer endowed our hearts with the capability to adjust its pumping actions to meet the changing demands on the body for energy. At the time of minimum bodily activity when the energy requirement of the body is low, the rate at which our heart beats is at its lowest. On the other hand, when the energy demand on the body increases, as during sporting activities, the rate at which our heart beats also increases.

Have you ever attended an athletic meeting to witness first-hand the first-class world athletes performing in the one hundred, two hundred, ten thousand metres, or perhaps the marathon? Even if you have not been able to attend such meetings personally, you are likely to have watched them on television. It is incredible what the heart is capable of achieving under such extreme conditions—fabulous, simply marvellous!

Our heart does its job automatically, without anyone's help, without anyone's battery to charge it, without anyone's fuel to power it, without anyone's oil to lubricate it. Even as we go through the emotion we call "broken heart," our dutiful heart neither breaks up nor goes on a break but instead keeps pumping, pumping, pumping.

Out of an incredible sense of duty, the heart placed in our chests by God the Righteous One pumps to sustain the lowest on the social ladder as well as those high up. The hollow muscular organ carries on its rhythmic contractions to pump blood to nourish the cells of an impoverished child going about in tattered clothes in parts of our world, as it does to keep the children of the super rich alive.

The heart is faithful to the homeless ones sleeping under bridges, parks and cemeteries in parts of our fallen planet, the same way it is to the millionaires and billionaires of our race as they rest in their luxurious homes.

Beyond the comprehension of an ordinary sinful mortal like myself, the heart designed by God Almighty pumps blood to sustain the lives of the atheists themselves. Yes, this includes even the hard-core amongst them, individuals who travel from continent to continent to cast insinuations at the Name of Him who is and evermore shall be. Is it incomprehensible? Indeed, but that is the nature of our loving Father God. Imagine if those denying God exists, walked in His shoes and had the power to dispatch His invisible angels, Michael for example, to earth at any time to do His bidding.

Let us pause to reflect. Let us for a second imagine *we* had the authority that is in the hands of the Supreme Commander of the Universe, God Almighty, He who called everything out of nothing, He who has the authority to do anything—and by anything, and I mean anything!

I am aware that these days, some, unfortunately including those who preach from the pulpit, belittle His power by spreading the falsehood that Almighty God stopped performing miracle long go. The fact that we cannot believe in His powers does not alter the fact that He is powerful beyond all belief and capable of doing anything He chooses, even at this very moment as you read these lines.

Let us for a moment imagine we could play God the Almighty. What would you and I, with our sinful hearts inclined towards avenging ourselves of those who step on our toes, do with such insolent, snotty-nosed beings of flesh and bones who go about not only heaping insults at us but also defaming our character?

I do not presume to speak for you, but the mortal man that I am; I would be inclined towards showing that impudent mass of flesh where real power lies. I would probably restrain my hands initially, but a time would soon come when I would likely say to myself, "Enough is enough!" I would then sign a Divine Decree to order the hearts I placed in those ungrateful chests—to pump blood to keep them alive—to cease from doing so with immediate effect. And so it would be, for the Word of the Almighty One does not proceed forth to the earth to return to Him empty, without it having accomplished what it was meant to accomplish.

At the moment the command is issued, the heart of Mr. Champion of Atheism, the expert boasting numerous titles, awards, and honours in Astrophysiology, Astrobiology, Astrochemicalogy, and Pharmacomedicology, the distinguished holder of the prize Nobelium, the Dean of the University of Excellence, while still on the podium receiving a standing ovation from an enthusiastic audience for an excellent speech on the accidental origin of life, would cease beating.

Without nutrients to sustain his sophisticated brain, he would pass out and collapse to the floor. Pandemonium would break loose as several of those assembled rush forward to offer first aid. Soon, they might hear in the distance the sirens of the ambulance speeding to the scene. The paramedics might do all in the power of mortal man to get the heart of the eminent man of letters restarted, but to no avail, for the Divine has decreed and so it shall be.

The mystery, however, is that God Almighty, the Creator of heaven and earth, does not act like you and me. What a huge heart He has! It is indeed unbelievable.

A muscular pump that works automatically to pump blood, to sustain us a lifetime beats my understanding. Pause a moment to think about it. Sit down to ponder over it, sister. Sit down to reflect upon it, men and women of the jury. How could such a construction have come about out of sheer chance?

Dear reader, you may be in a position to fathom it; perhaps you are able to imagine such a construction coming into existence out of pure chance. As far as I am concerned, however, it just beats my understanding. You may consider me naive, stupid, or regard me as a person living in delusion, but it cannot penetrate my mind!

Whatever others think about me, however, I will not move a millimetre from my standpoint. From deep inside the bottom of my heart, there is no way I can believe that the heart within me, the heart which dutifully pumps blood to supply oxygen and nutrients to my brain to give me the ideas to write what I am writing, could have come about as a result of an accident. It could not be the indirect result of an accidental big bang that occurred several billion years ago followed by a gradual evolution of the species from an original cell into humanity.

Many a highly regarded intellectual, among them Nobel Prize winners, may be able to believe such an absurd fallacy. As for me, I cannot.

Has too much learning made fools of us, to cause us to believe suddenly in chance evolution? Why, for heaven's sake, have we decided to throw common sense to the dogs?

Perhaps it is better to stop here before my emotions altogether carry me away, leading me to spend the rest of my days doing nothing apart from writing, writing, and once more writing in praise of the Awesome Designer of the universe!

Chapter 11
Our Milling Station

T hey meet at their conferences, heaping insults at the Creator God and at the end of the meeting gather around big tables to enjoy wonderful meals, the atheists of our race. Gathered around the dinner table with a rich supply of attractive dishes before them, I wonder if they for a moment think about the privilege they have to enjoy the products of Someone else's creation.

I wonder if they spare a minute to consider what use the plentiful supply of food before them would be to them had Almighty God not given thought to provide them with teeth to chew the food before them.

Yes, at the beginning of our earthly journey, when we arrived naked on earth, we did not possess teeth. The reason for this is not far-fetched—in the Divine plan, our body system was not ripe enough to handle solid food. He endowed our mothers with breasts to produce milk to sustain us. In the course of time, something extraordinary began to happen—we began to develop teeth! Soon we would begin to make use of solid food.

Now, back to the meal the honourable ladies and gentlemen vehemently denying the existence of God are enjoying.

The Divine Designer, being so good, supplied us food to feed on. He might have concluded that it would be unkind of Him to condemn us to a life feeding only on milk. Imagine how boring such an existence would be! So, He placed at our disposal the birds of the air, the beasts of the fields, the fish of the small and mighty rivers as well as the oceans, salmon, turkey, duck, beef, mutton; oh, how delicious. Not only that, but He instructed the plants to produce food for our consumption.

To avert a situation whereby we would sit before a heap of foodstuffs and not be in the position to make use of them, the Divine Designer equipped us with teeth to chew. Divine goodness went a step further to equip our mouths with organs of taste. For how could we determine whether the food we were enjoying was delicious without the presence of such organs?

The organs of smell in our nose would also help us, among other things, to determine not only that a particular meal was appealing, but also that it had gone bad and needed to be avoided.

How amazing is Divine goodness!

In the Divine plan, food is not only to provide us with energy but also to help us grow. In order for that to be possible, our bodies must fish out the nutrients hidden in the food, like treasures, through the sophisticated process of digestion. Papa God provided for that by supplying the body with chemicals to facilitate the process of digestion or breakdown of the food we eat. Saliva produced by glands in the mouth contains digestive enzymes that begin the breakdown of starchy food upon reaching the mouth.

After food has been broken down in the mouth through the chewing process, we swallow it down to the stomach. Wait a moment while I take you through another brilliant mechanism Papa God put in place in our bodies to facilitate swallowing. When I came to understand the anatomy of the throat and the functions the various structures found there play, I could only open my mouth in awe. At that moment I saw no option but to join King David in proclaiming: "I will praise thee;

for I am fearfully and wonderfully made: marvellous are thy works; and that my soul knoweth right well" (Ps. 139:14). Indeed, our body is wonderfully made!

I would like to present an illustration from day-to-day life to try to bring home the point I wish to convey. It is no secret that when a man and a woman first fall in love, they have the tendency to lose their heads for each other. During the initial stages of such a relationship, emotions can run high, with each of the two yearning only for the presence of the other. It is not for nought that someone came up with the saying, "Love is blind."

I remember at the time we were growing up, we boys used to write love letters to some of the girls growing up with us. Though it dates back several years, I still remember some of the wording. "I love you 99.999 percent. You add the 0.001 percent to complete the fairy tale!" "You are the honey of my life, the sweetness in the dreams of my silent nights!" There is nothing wrong with that, if only we allow things to proceed in line with Divine principles. I shall resist, however, any temptation to delve deeper into that area of human endeavour since it is not the issue at hand.

Gentleman A has met his lover, Lady A. As a way of impressing her, he invites her to a restaurant—African, Chinese, Indian, Italian, or what have you. Even as the meal is progressing, Mr. Freshly in Love is talking big and promising the love of his heart big things. A holiday on board the latest luxury liner is all but booked, he declares. It is to lead to a rendezvous on a romantic island in the Pacific, boasting tidy shores lined with blossoming palms. It is big, big talk!

As he makes his compelling promises, enjoying the rich meal before him, does he realise he owes his Maker a debt of gratitude for putting the appropriate mechanism in his throat to preserve him from an incident that could lead to his premature death—long before he could settle down and enjoy marital bliss with the dream of his life?

Yes, the principles behind the working of the structures built into our throat should be enough to dissipate any thoughts circulating in our minds concerning accidental evolution.

Allow me to offer a quick overview of how this part of our body functions. The trachea, or windpipe, leads to the lungs; the oesophagus, or gullet, leads to the stomach. The two tubes, windpipe and gullet, are close neighbours, the trachea lying in front of the oesophagus. The matter does not end here. The two structures are not only close neighbours; their openings converge at the same area in the throat.

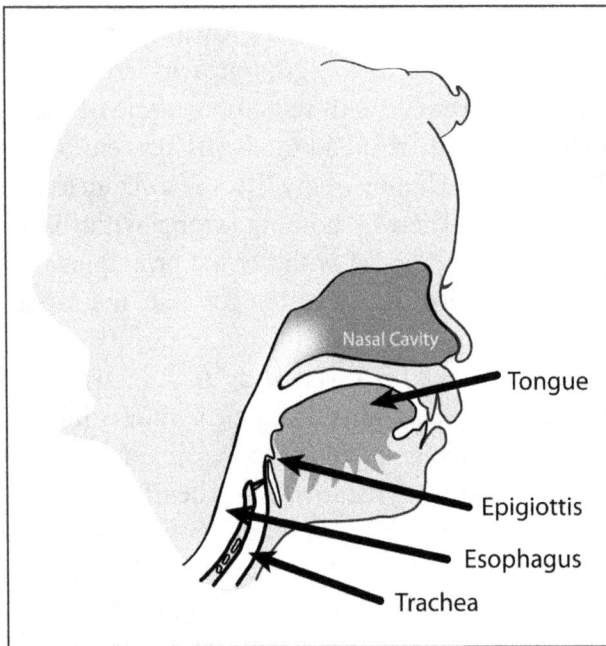

Fig. 7. The trachea (windpipe) and the oesophagus (gullet) are close neighbours, with the trachea lying in front of the oesophagus.

Whereas we might describe the relationship between the two structures as cordial, it is not free of problems. This is due to the characteristics of the two organs to which each of the two neighbours connect. The trachea leads to the lungs, while the oesophagus leads to the stomach. Whereas God created the stomach to deal with food and fluids, the lungs abhor food and liquids in the strongest terms. Indeed, the lungs need the strongest protection from its two sworn enemies, and failure to do so could have dire consequences.

To bring the picture close to home, I shall narrate a personal experience I had several months ago. On a particular day, accompanied by my two boys, I pulled up at a filling station to fill my tank. Thereafter, I drove about one hundred metres to the supermarket to which the filling station belongs to do some shopping. To my utter surprise, the engine would not start when I returned from the shop. It came as a surprise to me, because my car had until then been very faithful.

Eventually, I called for the emergency service. First, my rescuer tested the electrical system. Everything was in order. He was at a loss. Then he turned to me and asked, "Did you tell me you filled your tank shortly before the incident?"

"Yes," I replied.

"Are you sure you filled it with the right fuel?"

Initially I said yes, because I had always paid good attention to that.

"Are you sure?" he inquired.

I opened my wallet and pulled out the receipt. It came home to me. Yes, you guessed it; I had filled the tank with the wrong fuel! Distracted by my two boys who had been struggling with each other in the back seat, I had picked up the green tube at the station and fed unleaded petrol to my engine, instead of making use of the black tube to fill it with diesel. It was a costly mistake. Thank God, I had a comprehensive insurance policy in place so I did not have to pay on my own.

Just as the petrol led to the choking of the diesel engine, in the same way, as far as the lungs are concerned, food and water are a matter of life and death. The engineer who came to fix my problem told me petrol fed into a diesel engine carries more serious consequences than when it happens the other way round, i.e., when one fills diesel into a petrol engine. That is exactly the situation with the lung and the stomach. Whereas food and liquid that enters the lungs could lead to serious consequences, even death, the stomach can swallow considerable amounts of air without any harm.

Since we did not arrive here by chance, because the Great Designer of the universe created us, He made provisions to ensure the close proximity of the two structures to each other did not serve as a hindrance to the fulfilling of the respective roles He had assigned them. We would expect that an Intelligent Designer would take steps towards protecting the lung, the more sensitive of the two organs, from damage. That exactly is the case.

The Great Designer of the seen and unseen devised the epiglottis. He attached this flap of elastic cartilage to the root of the tongue to serve as a soldier to guard the opening leading into the lungs. It is normally pointed upward, but the moment food and liquids journey to the stomach, a complex neuromuscular activity involving the brain, the nerves, and the muscles forming part of the epiglottis, comes into play which results in the epiglottis moving into place to cover the windpipe. The food and the liquid then slide over it into the oesophagus, the gullet, thus avoiding the windpipe beneath! As a result, we sometimes refer to the epiglottis as the guardian of the airways. Give the Almighty God another round of applause!

Almighty God, aware that some of us, like the gentleman planning his extravagant cruise, have the tendency to brag or blow our horns before the whole world even during mealtimes, anticipated that our actions could lead to the failure of the protective mechanism spearheaded by the epiglottis. The reason for this situation is not far-fetched, for we also call the larynx the voice box; the two vocal cords that produce sounds when we speak are attached to part of the larynx. When we speak or sing, muscles pull these cords together. The air passing through the cords makes them vibrate to produce sounds that the brain interprets.

The same voice box or larynx forms the opening to the lungs, which the epiglottis is there to protect. It is a contradictory situation, isn't it? It is like when a father seeks to draw his teenage child away from danger, yet at the same time the teenager who seems to know better than everyone seeks to go his or her own way. The loving human father normally will not want the estranged child to go astray. If we who are sinners know what is good for our children, think about our loving Heavenly Father!

Almighty God placed an additional protective mechanism in place to prevent food, water, and other foreign objects from finding their way into our windpipe and causing damage to our lungs or choking us. He sought to achieve this by way of the gag or pharyngeal reflex, which leads to retching, as well as the cough reflex that aims at getting rid of foreign bodies that attempt to reach or have reached the windpipe.

When we brag, gossip, or have an accident during a meal, the protection accorded us by way of the epiglottis can fail. Food, drink, and other foreign objects threaten to damage the lungs, and the above reflexes come into play with the goal of averting the potentially dangerous situation.

If you happen to have an anaesthetist, a medical doctor who has specialised in the art of putting us to sleep during surgical procedures, as a relative or friend, you may ask that learned fellow to reveal to you some of the scenarios dreaded most in that speciality. You will surely hear that one of the most frightening scenarios in the field of medical practice is the situation when a patient's saliva or stomach contents find their way into the lungs during a surgical procedure. Having put the patient to sleep and having administered medication to relax the muscles, the anaesthetist has in effect put the protective action of the epiglottis, if temporally, out of service. If it gets into your lungs, the acidic contents of the stomach could cause an inflammatory reaction that could destroy the lungs and lead to death.

When we breathe, the epiglottis assumes its original position, directing air through the windpipe into the lungs. Some air may eventually find its way into our stomachs. That, as I mentioned earlier, is not serious for the digestive system, as it can cope with a certain amount of air that finds its way there. At worst, the limited volume of gases accumulating in the system can lead to embarrassment when all of a sudden, in a public place, an explosive sound emanates from our nether regions, leading all present to direct their eyes at us.

Digestion, which began in the mouth through chewing and mixing saliva with food, continues when food reaches the stomach. The stomach is another ingenious creation of the Divine Designer. He, with all certainty, did not place us on the planet to occupy all our time with eating. Let us imagine what life would be like if we had to return to our dining table every hour to feed ourselves because we could no longer tolerate our hunger pangs.

To avert a situation of that nature, the Creator placed a storage tank, the stomach, in our bodies. Filling it full suppresses our hunger pangs for a while and enables us to go about our activities without the need for food.

The stomach serves not only as a storage tank for food; it also plays a very important role in the digestive process. Through a process of rhythmic contraction movements termed peristalsis, it mechanically mixes the food that reaches it. It also produces hydrochloric acid that plays a key role in the digestive process by helping to break down proteins, fat, vitamins, and minerals.

The acidic milieu of the stomach helps kill bacteria, viruses, and parasites taken in with our food and water. In this regard, I can only be grateful to my stomach for the important role it played in my life as I grew up in rural Ghana. Devoid of clean drinking water, I had no choice but to daily take in water contaminated with millions, if not billions or trillions of microorganisms with the potential to cut short my stay on earth.

At regular intervals, the stomach propels its contents into the small intestine where the process of digestion continues. The pancreas and the small intestine release enzymes to help digest and absorb carbohydrates, fat, and protein. In addition, bile salts secreted from the gallbladder help with the digestion and absorption of fats and the fat-soluble nutrients, vitamins A, D, E, and K. From the small intestine, any undigested food passes to the colon or large intestine. By the time the product of the digestive process gets there, most of the nutrients have been absorbed, leaving indigestible fibre and water. Some water, electrolytes, and a few vitamins are still absorbed.

The waste product of digestion moves on to the last part of the large intestine known as the rectum. The rectum acts as a temporary storage facility. As its walls expand due to the material filling it, receptors from the nervous system located in its walls stimulate the desire to get rid of the products of digestion accumulating there. We normally act on it and relieve ourselves of the waste through the anus.

Before I leave this chapter, I shall say a few words on the matter of the anus. Throughout history, controversy has arisen concerning the function of the anus. That this should be the case reflects in my opinion the pathological state the human mind reverted to when humankind fell from grace to grass in the Garden of Eden long, long ago. The Bible says that with that fall came the knowledge of good and evil.

However, God Almighty did not leave us alone to wallow in that miserable state. Instead, He decided to send His only begotten Son, Jesus Christ, into the world to lead us back to Himself. I will deliberately not dwell on any details here, for doing so will forestall the import of this present discourse, not that I want to shy away from the issue. I will definitely return to it at the appropriate time. In the meantime, if you want to challenge me on the matter, we could arrange to meet over a cup of tea or coffee or chocolate drink if that is what you prefer.

Indeed, I believe deeply in my heart that in its very originality, Papa God ordained that our back passage should serve solely as an exit point for the expulsion of the waste products of the food we eat. I personally cannot figure out why the Supreme Commander of the universe would want to assign that structure any other function apart from the function already mentioned. What, after all, is *gay* about our back passage?

Chapter 12
The Glucose Regulator

I want to restate that I do believe wholeheartedly the account of the Bible that God Almighty created humankind and that at the beginning of creation, everything was perfect. Then came the Fall and with it human suffering, disease being one example.

Members of the medical profession spearheaded by doctors have taken it upon themselves to do all within the power of the human mind to heal disease and in so doing help alleviate human suffering. It is important for a doctor to be able to maintain a certain degree of emotional distance to the suffering of patients, as a safeguard from breaking down under the weight of human suffering seen on a regular basis.

The degree to which a doctor is able to come to terms with the problem of suffering depends of course on the individual involved. For me in particular, one aspect of suffering that especially pricks my heart as a doctor is seeing little children suffering from diabetes injecting themselves with insulin or pricking their fingers to check their blood sugar levels. The thought that such children would have to repeat the scene described a few times each day throughout their lives is enough to break even the heart made of steel.

As I have mentioned on several occasions in my presentation, we begin to appreciate the importance of the organs Almighty God has placed in our bodies to help us exist on earth only when things go wrong with them. What then has gone wrong in the body of the child who has to go through such a routine torture?

Almighty God placed us on the planet earth for a purpose. To go about our activities, we would need energy. He created plants and animals to provide us food. Through the process of digestion, the foodstuffs we eat are broken down into three basic components: glucose, amino acid, and fatty acid. These are eventually absorbed into our bloodstream.

We may consider glucose as a kind of fuel—petrol, diesel, or kerosene—that needs to be burned to power our body systems. For glucose to be effective, it must move into the cells to power the various reactions going on there.

To make that possible, Almighty God placed at our disposal the pancreas. Weighing approximately eighty grams, it is located behind the stomach. The pancreas serves two main functions. In the first place, it produces enzymes that help in the digestion of foodstuffs once they pass from the stomach into the small intestine.

Most importantly, however, it produces two substances—insulin and glucagons, that help to regulate the level of glucose in the blood. Without doubt, insulin, which helps to transport glucose from the bloodstream into the cells, is the more important of the two.

After we have eaten to our full and digestion and absorption has led to an elevation of the level of glucose in our bloodstream, the pancreas receives an order from the brain to release insulin into our bloodstream. The insulin so released picks up the glucose circulating in the bloodstream for onward transport into the cells, like the letter carrier picking up our letters from the post office and depositing them in our letterboxes.

By means of one stone, insulin, the pancreas seeks to kill two birds. Firstly, it reduces the concentration of sugar levels in the blood and by so doing averts the harm that such high concentrations could have on the body in the end. Secondly, insulin ensures that the glucose reaches the parts of the body that need it, mainly, inside the cells.

The pancreas is not a kind of inflexible robot that, once programmed, carries out its functions in only one direction. No, it is a very clever entity, our pancreas. The moment it detects a low sugar level in our blood, it ceases for a while from releasing additional insulin into the bloodstream. Should the blood sugar levels fall below a level that threatens to inhibit the working of the brain cells (indeed, the brain cells are very vulnerable to low sugar levels), the pancreas switches into reverse gear and triggers another type of cell within its own body, glucagons, into action.

Glucagon, we may call her the younger sister of insulin, plays exactly the opposite role as her elder sister. She immediately knocks on the door of the liver, the Glucose Bank of the body, and presents a cheque to purchase a specific amount of glycogen stored there (glycogen is the storage form of glucose). This is immediately broken down into glucose and placed at the disposal of the whole body. We can compare the mechanism to a situation where we keep our money in the form of gold bars in a bank. In the time of need, we withdraw our gold bars and convert them into physical cash.

In the person with Type I diabetes, the cells in the pancreas responsible for the production of insulin are destroyed. The problem with insulin is that when it is swallowed in the form of a tablet, it is destroyed in the digestive tract before it can be absorbed into the bloodstream; hence the need for it to be injected. There is a lot of research going on to produce forms of insulin that patients can inhale. Though scientists have made some breakthroughs, as of now the most feasible therapy for this type of patient is by way of insulin injection.

In Type II diabetes, a milder form of the disease, cells of the pancreas are still capable of producing insulin, though not in sufficient quantities. Such patients have to take tablets that among other things help to activate the remaining pancreatic cells to increase the production of insulin. Some of these patients may have to inject insulin in addition to taking the tablets.

Chapter 13
The Most Sophisticated
Factory on Earth

H uman beings over the centuries have come to regard the consumption of alcohol as a normal way of life. We consume alcohol on various occasions: before meals, during meals, after meals, during celebrations. In our joy for having won that game, that general election, the heart of that lady or gentleman of our dreams, we pick up a glass of wine and introduce alcohol into our body system—whether we consume a small amount or binge drink ourselves to the point of losing our sense of orientation. Though we may belong to the group of people who do not want to have anything to do with God Almighty, we had better go on our knees and give Him thanks for placing the liver in our body to detoxify or render harmless the poison, alcohol, that we have introduced into our body system.

What a fascinating organ is the liver! It is not only the largest organ inside our body; it is among the most, if not the most complex organ in the body. We could also count it among the most sophisticated factories on earth, if indeed it is not *the* most sophisticated factory on earth.

Humanity has built factories where we manufacture new goods and products. We have also erected factories such as oil refineries where dirty petroleum is refined, and water processing plants where we purify seawater, rich in salt, for human consumption. The liver is a factory that can combine both of these functions, namely the synthesis of new products for the body and the refinery or detoxification of impure substances in the body.

The liver weighs approximately 1.5 kg and lies in the upper right part of our abdomen. After we have eaten and the process of digestion is complete, the small intestine absorbs substances useful to the body. But the Great Designer took an important precaution. He would not allow the substances to pass indiscriminately into our bloodstream to cause possible damage to the body. Instead, He decided to channel all the newcomers to the body into a first assembly point for processing before introduction into the general body system. An intelligent arrangement, isn't it? It is like a country that directs all new arrivals at her borders through an immigration check in order to fish out illegal immigrants, spies, terrorists, and contraband goods being smuggled into the country.

A big blood vessel called the portal vein holds the responsibility of transporting absorbed items from the small intestine into the liver. On arrival of the products transported by the portal vein, the liver goes into immediate action. To get a clear picture of what I am explaining, one might picture a situation in a factory where a huge truck has just arrived to deliver goods for further processing. First, workers sort the items—amino acids to the right, glucose to the left, glycerol to the other corner, alcohol and other toxins to the farthest end of the hall! Thus goes the command from the supervisor of Factory Liver Complex.

Soon we see the manufacturing wing of Factory Liver Complex busy at work. Contrary to the attitude of some of us to waste all we have in times of plenty, the liver prepares the body for uncertain times, times when the body might be short of resources. As a precautionary measure, it goes into action to convert excess glucose, glycerol, and amino acids into their storage forms of glycogen, fatty acids, and protein respectively.

The synthetic wing of the liver manufactures other important products such as clotting factors.

As I mentioned earlier, the liver has purification and detoxification capabilities. Among the items the liver needs to detoxify are the medications we introduce into our bodies to help cure diseases, the impure substances that get into our body system via the air we breathe, the water we drink, and the food we eat, as well as those produced internally through chemical reactions taking place in our cells.

In this regard, I want to return briefly to the matter of alcohol.

As I have indicated, contrary to the false impression held by many of us, alcohol is not food for the body, but rather a kind of poison. Like any poison, it has the potential to destroy our body and send us to a premature death. True, the liver is there to detoxify the blood of toxins. As the old adage has it, however, too much of anything is bad. The same is true of the liver's ability to carry out alcohol detoxification.

Indeed, excessive consumption of alcohol can in the short or long run place an undue burden on the liver. The alcohol swimming in our system can adversely affect the liver, struggling to convert it into a form harmless to us, in several ways. First, it could inhibit the liver in its performance of other vital functions assigned it by the Almighty: the production of digestive enzymes, clotting factors, cells needed in the defence of the body.

These in turn could lead to impairment of the body's ability to absorb proteins, fats, and fat-soluble vitamins, as well as lower the defence capability of our body. Even more detrimental to the body, chronic alcohol consumption can damage the liver itself as fat deposits bring about what is known as fat liver and other organs such as the brain, pancreas and stomach.

The liver also plays a vital role in the production of bile. Here, again, there is a great deal of intelligence in design. Most of the waste products resulting from the activities of the liver pass on to the kidney for excretion. Not in the case of bile, however, which in the main is the by-product from the breakdown of the red blood cells in our body. Eventually these waste products end up in the gall bladder. The saying is one man's poison is another man's breakfast. It is true in this case. What is poison to our blood turns out to be breakfast for the digestive system. We need bile for the breakdown of the fat we eat, so Almighty God decided to store the waste product, bile, in the gall bladder. Whenever we eat fatty food and the fat gets into the small intestine, the small intestine first informs our command centre, our brain, about the latest development. The brain discharges an e-mail to the walls of the gallbladder, requesting it contract and discharge some of its contents into the small intestine to help break down fat. In real life, alliances and pacts are made and broken rampantly, but it is not so in our body. The Divine decreed that the various parts of our body cooperate with one another for our common good, and so it happens.

I hope this overview, though brief, has helped us appreciate the invaluable role of our liver in our lives. Should it decide to go on strike for any reason, our sojourn in this world will end within days, if not hours.

From our little insight into the role played by the liver in our lives, we can also understand why the attempts of the ingenious human mind to come up with a machine that can fully mimic its functions have so far proved futile.

Much as the best brains amongst us have tried in this regard, the farthest they have come is a kind of dialysis machine capable of assuming only part of the functions performed by the Liver Factory Complex.

Chapter 14
A Dutiful Filter

A nother organ of the body, whose function will blow our minds when we come to understand how it works, is the kidney. Those who, for one reason or the other, have non-functioning kidneys and as a result must rely on the dialysis machine, and to some extent those who operate such machines, will best appreciate the important role our kidneys play in our lives.

As we read above, our liver is a factory that synthesises and detoxifies several substances. As we also noted, some of the waste products resulting from the activities of the liver are stored in the gall bladder as bile. Some, like urea, pass on to the kidney for filtration from the bloodstream. Indeed, such waste products would poison our bodies within a few days, had the Rock of Ages not placed a pair of kidneys at our disposal to serve as filter stations to help rid our body of such waste.

Located at the bottom of our ribcage towards the back of our body, our kidneys are fist-sized, bean-shaped, and dark red in colour, each weighing around 130 grams or one quarter of a pound.

One quarter of our blood supply passes through them every minute. Whilst in the kidney, the blood visits minute filtration units known as nephrons. Each kidney possesses around one million nephrons. Water, salts, acids, alkalis and in particular urea, which are breakdown products of the protein we eat, are filtered from the blood.

Depending on the needs of the body, the blood absorbs some of the filtered substances as they pass through the kidney on their way to collecting points to leave the body eventually as urine.

Apart from the above functions, the kidneys help regulate our blood pressure and play a role in the production of red blood cells. The details as to how the kidney carries out these functions are better left to the experts.

Before I leave the kidneys, I would like to pass some comments with regard to their main function, namely the filtration of waste products from the blood. As I have mentioned on several occasions in this book, we have the tendency to take our body functions for granted until something goes wrong. Then, the important role a particular part of the body plays in our lives begins to dawn on us. That is very true of our kidneys. Indeed, every day, our kidneys help rid our bodies of loads of poisonous waste material without us taking any note of it. It is when something goes wrong to either restrict their ability to perform or prevent them from performing altogether that the awareness suddenly dawns on us, sometimes in dramatic fashion.

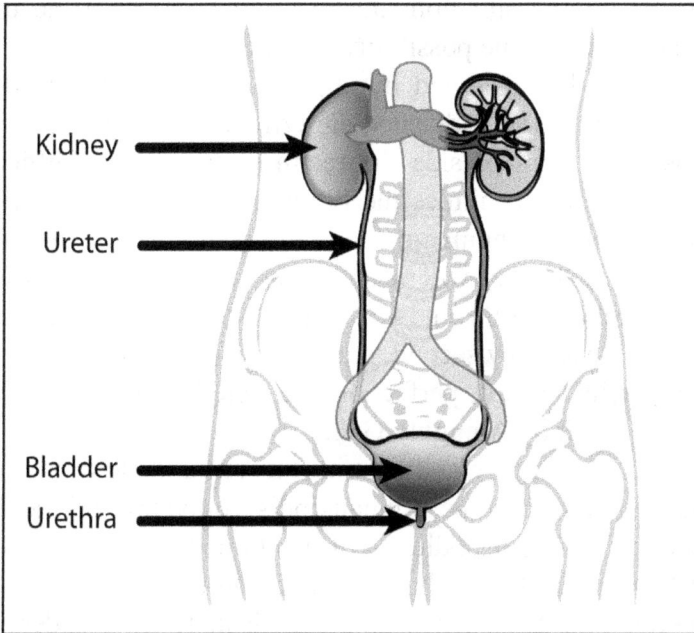

Fig. 8. Urine produced in the kidneys passes to the bladder, a hollow, collapsible, muscular sack located a distance beneath the kidneys, behind the pelvic bone, for storage.

What options does a person experiencing complete kidney failure have at their disposal?

In several areas of the world, that scenario would be tantamount to a death sentence. For example, an individual living in a place like Amantia, the village in Ghana where the eyes of my mother first saw the light of day, would have to hurry up to divide her property amongst family members if she had not done so already in anticipation of the imminent end.

Elsewhere on the globe, where better conditions of life than those found in little Amantia prevail, depending on the medical condition that has led to the situation, doctors might resort to the dialysis machine or consider the possibility of a kidney transplant.

Yes, the brilliant human mind has come up with the dialysis machine. To provide a detailed description of how the machine functions would fall outside the realm of this book. Suffice it to know, dear reader, it mimics the filtration activity of the kidney. A comparison between human-made dialysis and the original dialysis machine made in heaven will make it clear to us where real power lies.

To start, let us picture our two healthy kidneys, lying in our bodies, carrying out, second by second, minute by minute, hour by hour, day by day, and with absolute perfection, the incredible blood purification role assigned to it by Almighty God.

Next, let us compare and contrast this remarkable pair of organs with the dialysis machine, humankind's equivalent of the Divine filtration station in our bodies. As I mentioned, each kidney weighs around 130 grams. The dialysis machine, on the other hand, weighs several kilograms. Still, by way of comparison, let us consider the cost involved in acquiring, running, and maintaining the dialysis machine, not neglecting the cost of energy, material, and personnel required to run the machine. Furthermore, let us consider the inconveniences the person who relies on the dialysis machine has to bear—the two or three weekly excursions to a dialysis centre, the injections endured, the two-to-four hour dialysis session, not to mention the discomfort experienced during the sessions—nausea, vomiting, cramps, back pain, and more.

Finally, to prevent the blood from clotting as it passes through the machine, the patient regularly must take medication aimed at suppressing the body's clotting mechanism. Whereas this state of affairs is desirable to permit the dialysis process, it is not without risk to the patient; such a patient lives with the risk of excessive blood loss in case of injury.

In light of the comparison we have drawn between man-made dialysis and the solution manufactured in heaven, does it not represent a blatant disrespect to the honour and dignity of the Chief Engineer of creation—the Power behind all that is seen and unseen—to refuse honour where honour is due and deny the existence of the Master of all creation?

We go about collecting prizes for inventing the dialysis machine. Only when it comes to the Dialysis made in heaven do we begin to talk about chance evolution!

It boils down to intellectual corruption of the highest degree!

Chapter 15
An Intelligent Water Storage Tank

I am beginning to lose count of the intelligent designs built into our body system to ensure its smooth function. The principle behind the urinary bladder is without doubt one of the wonders at work in our body. You and I, let us sit down to ponder what our lives would be like should the urine formed in the kidneys have to pass directly out of our bodies. Let us imagine that God did not endow us with a storage station for urine, and that we had to pass urine all the time!

Almighty God, the intelligent Designer behind our being, devised a storage station within the body where we could store urine, allowing us to go about our activities until the need to discard it arrived.

Urine produced in the kidneys thus passes on to the bladder, a hollow, collapsible, muscular sack located beneath the kidneys, behind the pelvic bone, for storage.

The Great Designer did not make the bladder a kind of robot that is unresponsive to change. No, even in the matter of an ordinary storage tank for urine, the Great I Am decided to provide a considerable degree of intelligence by placing several sensitive nerves within its walls. An adult bladder normally can comfortably hold about a pint or a half litre of urine. As it fills and stretches beyond a certain point, the sensitive nerves relay messages to the brain, informing it to do something before it is too late.

We may try to suppress this urge for a while, but sooner rather than later, the tension on the walls builds to the extent that it causes the nerves to stretch and stretch. The nerves, angered by our impudence in neglecting their call for action, begin to tune their signals to the brain into a form that makes us feel the pinch. Soon, the driver on the highway, who in an attempt to beat a deadline had so far refused to heed the instruction emanating from below, has no choice but to stop at the next convenient place to ease the torment coming from the water storage tank.

Urine leaves the body by flowing out of the bladder down a tube called the urethra. To ensure urine leaves the body under some control even when the bladder is at the point of bursting, the Ancient of Days put into place at the junction between the bladder and urethra a bundle of muscles known as a sphincter, and entrusted it with an open-and-close function.

If, like the driver above, we decide that the time has come for us to empty our bladder of urine, our brain sends a command to the sphincter to order it to relax. The sphincter obeys, leading the bladder-urethra junction to open up. At that moment the bladder contracts, to force the urine down the urethra and out of our body.

Only those who have shut their eyes to reality for reasons best known to themselves will fail to recognise the hands of a Designer in such a brilliant construction.

Chapter 16
Almighty God Supplying Free Air for All

H ave you ever been in a situation of near suffocation? Perhaps you dived into water and stayed under a few minutes to test your endurance.

It brings to mind memories of the time when I was growing up in little Mpintimpi. During weekends and school holidays, after we had returned from work on our farms, our parents would ask us, the young ones, to head for the Nwi River, about a mile away, to fetch water for use at home. We collected the water in buckets made of plastic or aluminium and carried them back home on our heads. Often, after we had done a few rounds, we spent time swimming in the river before finally returning home.

I remember times when some of us teenage boys seized the opportunity to carry out acts we considered brave and which we designed to impress the girls accompanying us. I would not advise anyone reading this to emulate our example. What did we do? Well, though it happened several years ago, it is still vivid in my memory. We dived underwater and sought to remain there as long as we could. During that time, one of us would count from one upwards until the candidate emerged from the water. He who stayed longest won the day.

Much as we wanted to stay underwater as long as possible, we realised after a few minutes, if not seconds, that God Almighty did not create us as fish, but humans capable only of breathing oxygen under the conditions on land. Some members of our race through training are capable of staying underwater longer than we did. Even people with such extraordinary capabilities soon discover their limitations in their desire to live like a fish.

Now let us assume for the sake of our present discussion that air, atmospheric oxygen, the essential of all essentials needed to sustain our life, is not free; by free I really do mean free—not the kind of gift with strings attached. Let us assume we buy and sell air like any other commodity.

Indeed, let us picture in our minds momentarily that life-sustaining air, though abundant, is subject to free market, the rules of the capitalist system. In fact, let us assume air is a commodity listed on the international stock market, on the New York, Frankfurt, London, or Tokyo Stock Exchange.

The English, in pondering such a scenario, may probably react with a scream of, "God forbid!" The German may exclaim, "Du Meine Gute!" The Twi speaking Ghanaian may in exasperation cry, "Nyame mpa ngu!"

Putting in human hands the trade in life-sustaining air is unthinkable! One thing I know for sure is if that were the case, I would not be sitting behind my desk on this February trying to put my thoughts together. With all certainty, my bones would by now be resting peacefully in a grave at the outskirts of little Mpintimpi. I would probably have made it to year two in the local primary school; nothing beyond that, friends, nothing beyond that. Much as my impoverished parents would have wished to keep me alive, they would not have been able to afford to pay for a continuous supply of oxygen to ventilate my lungs beyond my tenth birthday.

I hear someone at the other end of the street say that in view of the extreme importance of oxygen to life on earth, the human race would have for once shown compassion and mercy in their dealings with it. That person seems to be suggesting that in view of the extraordinary role air plays to sustain life on earth, human life included, humanity would for once have allowed compassion, pity, fellow-feeling to guide their dealings with one another. In this particular instance at least, the principle of "love your neighbour as yourself" would be paramount in the thinking of all of us, I am told.

I beg to differ. I base my scepticism, if you wish to use that word to describe my attitude, on the way and manner in which society has so far handled the two other vital necessities of life, water, and food.

I shall spare my readers a detailed lecture on the issue of hunger and starvation in our world in the face of abundance. I will restrict myself to a single example.

Recently I watched a TV documentary that showed how fishermen from the European Union, after they had laboured on the high seas to catch fish, at the end of the day dumped large quantities of their catch—fish dead after staying out of water for a while—back into the seas. I saw the report with my naked eye, and I do not have reason to doubt its authenticity. According to the report, they did so in order to meet EU fishing quotas aimed at stabilising the price of fish in the EU.

Imagine that, friend. Fish that Almighty God called into existence, fish that grew in the ocean at no one's expense, fish fed day-by-day by Divine order. We take our boats and nets to harvest where we have not sown, and when by His grace we have had a good catch, we dump a considerable amount of the catch, dead after having disturbed their rest, back into the ocean!

Amazingly, it is conceivable to see the same individuals who set the rules that result in such despicable acts pointing accusing fingers in the direction of God Almighty when they see starvation on TV.

Almighty God in His absolute wisdom decreed that, in case of life-sustaining air, every member of His creation—the royal, the commoner, the millionaire, the desperately impoverished, believers, and avowed atheists heaping insults at His Holy Name—should have free access. Providing free oxygen to ventilate the lungs of your avowed enemy shows that the love of God surpasses all human understanding.

Some, while not denying the existence of God, have the audacity to say things like, "Leave me alone to do whatever I think fit. After all, it is *my* life!" How dare we allow such words to pass our lips! Do we for a moment imagine that our life is our own? We may indeed own the house we live in. Ownership of our property in my opinion is even conditional; we may call it our own until the next earthquake sets in to knock it to the ground.

But to think that our life is ours, in my opinion, is tantamount to spitting in the face of God Almighty. How can we claim possession of something when we have no control over the most vital, the vital of vitals, the air itself, needed to keep us alive?

Almighty God, responsible for the origin of all that is seen and unseen in the universe, decreed that so long as He allows the earth to exist in this present form, air will remain free. It will remain free from the manipulation of market forces, free from the manoeuvring of big politics, free from the evil intentions of wicked dictators who might otherwise cut off the supply and cause annihilation of the human race.

The proponents of evolution want us to believe life developed here by chance after oxygen formed through the big bang. In the same vein, they want us to believe the complex mechanism of breathing came about out of accident.

As far as I am concerned, such way of thinking boils down to asking someone to take a dip in the river and stay under forever because chance will adjust the functions of his or her lungs to cope with life there.

The truth is we are wonderfully made by a great and intelligent Designer! He planned everything carefully and executed it with absolute perfection. Not only did He place air at the disposal of all and sundry, He put the mechanism in place to ensure that our bodies are able to utilise the free air at our disposal.

Resting comfortably in Mama's womb, we did not need to breathe; instead, we drew from the oxygen in her blood and discarded the carbon dioxide we produced into her blood.

Almighty God activates our breathing mechanism shortly after we emerge from mother's womb and become exposed to the conditions on earth. The breathing mechanism springs into action. So it was with our fathers, so it is now, and so it will be so long as the Creator permits things to remain in the present state. The moment it ceases to function in an individual, that person leaves the ring of life.

The mechanism of breathing in itself is a wonder. The Master of creation placed an automatic centre within our brains to control the process. We do not have to think about breathing—it just goes on. The centre controlling that vital function of life has the capability even to override our own will power. Thus, when for a while decide to hold our breath, the control centre of respiration soon overrides our actions and forces us to resume breathing and the breathing process continues in us, anywhere between fifteen and twenty-five times per minute.

For the surrounding air to enter into the lungs, the pressure in our lungs should fall below that prevailing in the atmosphere. The lungs achieve this is by way of the expansion and by expansion of the chest cavity as a whole. Conversely, for the air in the lungs to press out into the atmosphere, the pressure in the lungs should exceed that of the atmosphere. This also occurs by way of the compression of the chest cavity and the lungs.

Air comes in through the nose. Usually the temperature of the outside is lower than that of the body. As it passes through the nose and the throat, the air warms. It is also filtered of impure substances contained in it. When the air reaches the lungs, a sophisticated network system called the alveoli facilitates its absorption into the bloodstream. The blood enriched with oxygen returns to the heart from which it pumps to other parts of the body.

At the same time this occurs, blood laden with carbon dioxide pumps back into the lungs. The carbon dioxide then diffuses from the blood into the air spaces, from where we breathe it out into the atmosphere.

Someone may believe that chance could have put such a system in place. As for me, I continue to believe wholeheartedly that only an intelligent Designer, God Almighty, could have come up with such a perfect and well-thought-out system.

Chapter 17
Eye of Faith

W hat a complex organism is the eye! When we were children, we played a game known as "Jack, Where Are You." It was a game two or more people could play. First, we blindfolded one of the players. Then we left the blindfolded person alone to try to catch one of us. To help the person locate us, each of us shouted, "Jack, where are you? I am here. Jack, where are you? I am here," while we moved around to avoid him. Although the blindfolded person sometimes managed to get hold of one of the players, he or she was severely handicapped with covered eyes and completely disoriented and helpless. How many accidents have occurred because we did not see? In the same way, how many accidents have we avoided because we recognised the danger at the last minute?

At the time I was growing up, one of the scenarios I dreaded most was a confrontation with a snake. Indeed, the danger was real. Contrary to the situation of my peers who lived in areas of the world devoid of snakes, we who lived at Mpintimpi were in real danger of being bitten by them. So, whenever we went to work on the farm I was always on the watch for the dreadful crawling reptiles of creation.

When I eventually came across one, I took to my heels at the fastest of speeds, never mind if the distance between human and reptile was considerable. I did not wait to categorize the danger. As far as I was concerned, so long as the danger was within visual (seeing) distance, it was enough reason for me to run for my life. How could I have assessed the danger to my life without the help of my eyes?

Though others have drawn capital from the look of their eyes; though many songs have been written and sung in adoration of the alluring look in the eyes of my dear one, Almighty Father put these sense organs in place in our bodies to help us appreciate His creation and enable us to find our way during our sojourn here.

For double security, He equipped us with a pair of eyes, so that should something go wrong with one, we could still rely on the remainder. He might as well have placed three, four, or even more eyes at our disposal. I personally think He settled for two for aesthetic reasons, to reflect on our design, apart, of course, from improving our depth vision or our perception of perspective.

In any case, who am I, the creature, to dictate to the Creator how He should go about designing His creation? Even in our day, we talk of artistic freedom. A free society allows its painters, authors, and sculptors the freedom to express themselves within the norms of a civilised society. In any case, at the end of the day, Almighty God settled on a pair of eyes.

Rays of light reach the eye through the opening, the iris. The iris is capable of adjusting its size to correspond to the intensity of light reaching it; it is widely open when the source of light is dim; when the light is even less intense, the iris opens wider still. When the light is bright, the aperture of the iris is much smaller.

The light from an object, after passing through the iris, passes through the lens, which focuses it upside-down on the retina, which we can describe as a screen. The retina contains highly light-sensitive structures known as rods and cones. Each retina is equipped with approximately one million such structures. The fibres from the rods and cones join to form the optic nerve that transmits the nerve impulses to an area at the back of the brain for interpretation.

If disease causes this visual part of the brain to lose its function, though our eyes remain perfect functionally, we will still not be able to see because the brain will not be able to interpret the signals reaching it from the eyes.

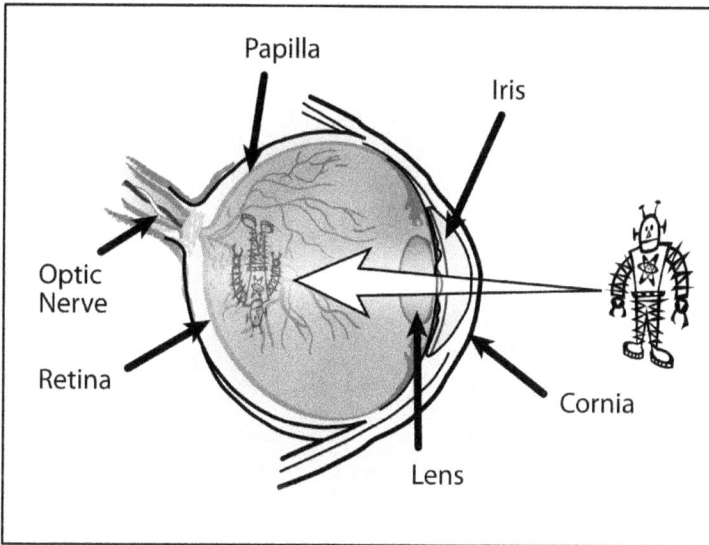

Fig. 9. Light from an object, after passing through the iris, passes through the lens to be focused upside down on the retina, which can be described as a screen.

Chapter 18
A Balancing Act

૬૨

T he ear is another sophisticated organ that only the hand of a
genius could have constructed. It is not only responsible for
hearing; it also helps us to maintain our balance.

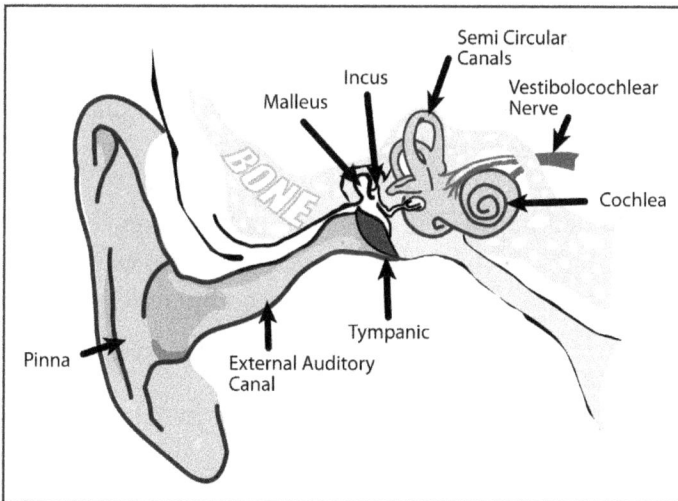

Fig. 10. The ear is made up of three parts: the outer, the middle, and the inner
ear. Sound waves travel through the ear canal to strike the tympanic membrane
(eardrum), causing it to vibrate. The vibrations are passed on to a system of three
small bones located in the middle ear and eventually to the brain.

The ear contains three parts: the outer, middle and inner ear. The fine details as to how it transmits sound waves to the brain are so complex that we had better leave them to the experts. For our discussion, it is sufficient to know that sound waves travel through the ear canal to strike the eardrum, causing it to vibrate. The vibrations pass on to a system of three small bones located in the middle ear. The small bones form a system of interlinked mechanical levers. The vibrations reach the hammer, the first of the three bones. The hammer then pushes on the second bone, the anvil, which in turn pushes on the third little bone, the stirrup.

The base of the stirrup rocks in and out against an oval window, which leads to a fluid system known as perilymph. The perilymph in turn transmits the vibrations to another fluid system, endolymph, which in turn causes the movement of hair cells of the organ of Corti.

The movement of the cells converts the vibrations into nerve impulses, which the acoustic nerve transmits to a specific area of the brain capable of interpreting the impulses as sound.

While it is complex, I have done my best to explain it in simple language. How, indeed, could such an intricate system have arrived in our heads from nowhere?

As mentioned before, the ear is not only responsible for hearing but also for helping us maintain our balance when we walk.

Should you visit your doctor one day complaining of difficulty in keeping your balance and of wanting to vomit, he or she might tell you your symptoms are due to labyrinthitis.

"What in the world does that terminology mean, Doc?!" You may ask him or her.

In reply, the physician will tell you the culprit may be an inflammation of a complex labyrinth-like structure in your inner ear that helps you keep your balance when you walk.

Indeed, when that labyrinth-like structure in the inner ear becomes inflamed, the balance maintained by the complex structure is disturbed. When we walk, we feel like falling down.

That mere chance could have put into place such a sophisticated system that, amongst others, helps us maintain the orientation of our bodies in space, keeps our posture and sense of balance, regulates our movements, and focuses visually while our bodies are in motion, is something that beats my understanding.

Chapter 19
The Most Sophisticated Defence Force on Earth

W e generally hold that the Chinese army boasts the largest number of soldiers, whereas the U.S. army is the most sophisticated and powerful on earth—this is far from the truth! It may come as a surprise to you, but without a shadow of doubt, the human body, the body that houses you and me is the most powerful protective army on earth, surpassing the Chinese army in numbers and that of Uncle Sam in ingenuity and sophistication.

We would fully appreciate this statement if we could glimpse the microscopic world to get an idea of the millions, perhaps billions, of microscopic organisms constantly attempting to invade our bodies to cause havoc.

It may sound macabre, but to appreciate the role played by the formidable Army Humanicus in sustaining our lives, let us sit down to consider what happens to our bodies when we die, when the soul dwelling in us gets the order to call it quits and depart from our physical body, when the heart stops beating and breathing ceases. When the Generals commanding our body defences sign a decree to urge the entire military establishment to lay down arms, the order is immediately executed. It is a unilateral cease-fire.

For sure, the bacteria, viruses, and parasites of the atmosphere do not lay down their arms because our Defence Forces have been compelled to do so. Unchallenged by our body's gallant combatants, the aggressive invaders pounce on us from all sides to party on our bodies. Like hungry lions in search of food, they tear our bodies apart and set about to mercilessly devour us. In the end, only our bones remain.

The HIV infection painfully brings home the important role played by our body defence system in sustaining us. Usually the invaders to our body direct their onslaught against various parts of our body system. The soldiers guarding our body then go into action to resist the invaders. In the case of HIV infection, the whole body is not subject to attack. Instead, the invaders direct their attack solely against the soldiers guarding our body complex.

We might compare the situation to that of a powerful army guarding a city. The fame of the army in question is legendary. Indeed, the very mention of the name of Army Powerful is enough to send shock waves down the spine of every soldier of the armies bordering on it.

Then something happens: a mysterious disease strikes the Army Powerful and leaves every soldier of the fearsome unit paralysed from the waist downwards. Soon news spreads to the neighbouring cities: "The Army of our formidable neighbour is incapacitated by disease! Come on! Let us go and avenge ourselves of past defeats and humiliations!" And they go about shouting the warning.

The human body is constantly under attack. A multitude of bacteria, microbes, viruses, toxins and parasites with varying modes of attack and differing systems of weaponry unceasingly assault us. Even as you are reading these lines, hordes of germs are busy seeking to penetrate your body.

Readers who have grown up in the part of God's planet referred to by many as the First World may not appreciate fully what I am attempting to explain. On the other hand, those who grew up under less hygienic conditions prevailing on the surface of the earth do not need a lecture from me to appreciate what I am trying to convey.

When I was growing up in my little African village our source of drinking water was, among others, the Nwi River. Should we today take a sample of this flowing river to a laboratory to have its microbe content per millimetre of water analysed, those viewing the sample under their microscope will have no other alternative than to congratulate my body defences for a job well done in preserving me against such a formidable force!

Of course, there were times when the military establishment in me became so overwhelmed by the great numbers of invaders attacking from all directions that it had to concede defeat. Defeat manifested itself as diarrhoea, vomiting, malaria, chest infection, and more. However, overall, my defence system succeeded in warding off the overwhelming proportion of attacks.

Someone will ask me, "Why did Almighty God expose us to such organisms in the first place?" I do not wish to answer that question. How can I, mortal man that I am, read the mind of the Almighty? I will attempt an explanation based on the understanding of my limited human mind. I shall repeat, the explanation that follows represents my own thinking and one may accept or reject it. I believe sincerely that when God Almighty first created Adam and Eve, there was no need for such a defence system. I believe that prior to the fall of humanity, humankind did not have the need of a body defence system, for we lived in harmony with God and His created world: "And God saw everything that he had made, and behold, it was very good" (Gen. 1:31a).

Then came the fall and the subsequent pronouncement of Divine judgement:

> And unto Adam he said, Because thou hast hearkened unto the voice of thy wife, and hast eaten of the tree, of which I commanded thee, saying, Thou shalt not eat of it: cursed is the ground for thy sake; in sorrow shalt thou eat of it all the days of thy life;
>
> Thorns also and thistles shall it bring forth to thee; and thou shalt eat the herb of the field; In the sweat of thy face shalt thou eat bread, till thou return unto the ground; for out of it wast thou taken: for dust thou art, and unto dust shalt thou return. (Gen. 3:17–19)

With the curse came human suffering and, worst of all, death. Even then, God Almighty did not leave us alone, but rather put into place in our body a defence system to help us cope with the hazards we would encounter during the period of our stay on the fallen planet.

I wish to reiterate that this explanation is borne out of my own fantasy; you are free to accept it or reject it.

After the fall of man, Almighty God in His goodness placed a defence system in place in our bodies to keep us well equipped to deal with the mayhem set loose on planet earth.

Again, I shall leave the fine details as to how our body defence system works to the experts. I will provide only a brief overview of the awesome defence force on guard duty around the clock in our body to defend us from invaders.

In the same way the army of a country consists of several units like the Air Force, Marines, and Ground Combat Battalions, Army Humanicus, developed in heaven for our common good, consists of several units with differing responsibilities.

We may compare our body to a walled city. Soldiers are on duty around the clock at the entry points or gates leading into the city, to guard it from possible invaders. The nose, mouth, and eyes are examples of possible entry points for germs into our body. The body has made provision for this by posting several soldiers to such points to fight potential invaders. Tears produced by our eyes contain enzymes capable of breaking down the cell walls of bacteria. Saliva produced by glands in our mouth is capable of destroying bacteria found in food. Mucus coats the walls of the nose and lungs. The mucus traps and kills some of the bacteria heading for the body and in doing so protects it from possible harm.

Our skin, the main wall to the city of our body, functions as a tough physical barrier that protects our body from damage and drying out, and is generally impermeable to bacteria and viruses. This is achieved by way of keratin, an exceptionally tough protein. Besides that, it secretes antibacterial substances that destroy bacteria that land on its surface.

Almighty God endowed our skin with the capability to protect us from the harmful effects of the rays of the sun. This is achieved by way of melanin produced by cells in the skin known as melanocytes. Melanin, the brown substance that gives colour to our skin, is capable of absorbing the sun's ultraviolet rays, which could otherwise cause harm to our body.

Despite the strength of the soldiers on guard duty on the entry points to our body and the toughness of skin, the mighty concrete wall surrounding us, many malicious attackers still manage to penetrate our bodies. For example, a cut, scratch, or bruise could serve as an entry point for all sorts of bacteria, viruses, and parasites.

Whether we like it or not we need to breathe so long as life lasts. In so doing, we must inhale thousands of bacteria and viruses floating in the air on a daily basis. Beside that, we regularly inhale all sorts of pollutants in the air resulting from our activities on earth.

The saying has it that a hungry man is an angry man. In the same manner, a hungry mosquito, somewhere in the tropics, in dire need of dinner for the day, may ferociously pounce on a human being who has retired to bed to rest for the day and suck his or her precious blood. In the process, the parasite could introduce potentially death-bringing plasmodium into the body of its victim.

The factors just alluded to, coupled with the sheer numbers of microscopic organisms and other foreign substances permanently seeking to invade, have the effect that in real life some of the organisms regularly succeed in outwitting our external defences.

This is where our immune system—we might call it our Internal Defence Force—comes into play. Like the clotting of blood, the fine details of how the immune system works is so complicated that we had better leave it to the experts. I will present only a brief summary here. In this regard, I will single out the role played by the white blood cells in this complicated system initiated in heaven for the good of sinful man. The white blood cells fall into three classes: granulocytes, which in turn are divided into three classes (neutrophils, eosinophiles, and basophils), lymphocytes (classified into B- and T-cells), and monocytes, which mature into Macrophages.

For the sake of simplicity, I shall restrict myself to the role played by the lymphocytes, the principal active components of the adaptive immune system in the body's military establishment. Those who have done a detailed study of the lymphocytes tell us there are about one trillion each of T- and B-cells circulating in the blood at any particular time.

A typical B- or T-cell possesses around one hundred thousand receptors on its membrane or surface that enable it to recognize specific antigens or attackers. The receptors are like grooves that fit patterns formed by the atoms of the attacking agent like a key fits a lock. In this way, the lymphocyte can bind to the invader and destroy it. The lymphocytes are equipped with more than 10 million types of grooves; in other words, they have about 10 million locking systems to deal with the various kinds of attackers to the body.

Let us ponder over this for a moment: one trillion lymphocytes, each possessing approximately one hundred thousand receptors, each receptor possessing millions of grooves to bind to germs and other foreign bodies attacking the body!

To maximize the chances of encountering attackers to the body wherever they might invade, lymphocytes continually circulate between the blood and lymphoid tissues, the spleen, lymph nodes, and the thymus. One might compare the situation to a soldier charged with defending a city leaving the barracks, the lymphoid tissues, to go on patrol in the environment in search of invaders to the city.

How does a white blood cell on patrol duty in the body identify the enemy or know who to attack and who not to attack? Like the situation on the street of any major city in a globalised world, the soldiers on patrol duty through our body are likely at any time to meet with citizens and foreigners within the city. On our streets, foreigners may be welcomed. This is not so when it comes to our body. As far as our Internal Defence Force is concerned, anything not identified as being one of us must without delay be attacked and rendered harmless—if need be, hacked to death. Our immune system does not take chances when it comes to invaders to our body. It will not give invaders the chance to settle comfortably in our home and take advantage of our hospitality before turning their weapons against us.

We should adopt the same attitude when it comes to temptation. Instead, we have the tendency to parley with it, tolerate it, compromise with it, until it grabs us by the throat one day and squeezes and squeezes and squeezes until no more life remains in us. Our body's defence system is not so compromising. It seems to operate according to the motto: "I will get you before you get me!"

Almighty God made provision to ensure that soldiers of the Internal Defence Force recognise strangers to the city while identifying its citizens. This is in the form of what we know as the Major Histocompatibility Complex (MHC), also known as the Human Leukocyte Antigen (HLA). As the name suggests, the MHC is a complex system. It comprises a set of molecules present on the surfaces of cells found in the body of an individual that marks the cells as belonging to the body of that particular person. Anything the immune system finds that does not have these markings (or that has the wrong markings) is definitely not that individual and is therefore fair game for the defence force.

We may compare it to the situation where a country equips her citizens with ID cards, leaving the police to arrest any individual on the street not so equipped. They automatically consider such persons illegal immigrants. Can you, dear reader, imagine chance coming up with such a brilliant, sophisticated mechanism aimed at protecting our bodies against invaders? You may be in a position so to do; I personally cannot!

These days, in certain parts of the globe, we tend to place emphasis on high standards of hygiene. I am aware that it may sound odd to read what will soon follow from someone who has spent considerable time with the medical academics. Still, I dare express myself, though my views may turn out to be unpopular.

I think that we sometimes overemphasize matters of hygiene. For example, I have read of mothers who disinfect everything around, going to the extent of placing a sterile shield around their breasts before breastfeeding their children. Do we need to go to that extent? Indeed, a certain degree of exposure to microorganisms is acceptable. For one thing, our defence system usually needs a challenge to keep in top form. Just as an army that does not enter into battle has a tendency to become soft, in the same way a bodily defence force needs a certain degree of engagement to remain in top gear. We might compare the situation to the military force of a country that by virtue of being surrounded on all sides by hostile countries is provoked on a regular basis into war to defend its borders. Being constantly under threat of attack and having to fight battles on a regular basis, its army is not only resilient but permanently battle-ready.

Before I leave the discussion on Army Humanicus, I shall make a short observation. Experts have observed that bitterness, an unforgiving spirit, anger, worry, hatred, or negative thoughts, if harboured for long, have a detrimental effect on the effectiveness of our defence system to protect us against invaders. Thus the Divine admonition to us to among other things love our neighbours as ourselves, learn to forgive our enemies, cast our burdens on the Lord and not to be anxious about tomorrow, at the end of the day, is medicine not only to our soul but also our body.

I humbly do submit, dear reader, members of the jury on the case in hand, only an Intelligent Designer could place such a terrific defence system in our body. Others may want us to believe the system came about out of pure chance, a mere adaptation of our bodies to cope with our exposure to dangerous and invasive organisms. If that is the case, why, for example, have the bodies of those who wish to live on this planet forever not adapted themselves to overcome death? It is no secret that, despite the earth's present chaotic state, some people wish to live here forever. If we are indebted to chance for everything seen and unseen in the universe, we might as well appeal to it to help us live here forever.

This reminds me of those who go about spreading falsehoods that we may one day, through our own making, live forever. In anticipation of such a scientific breakthrough, some members of our race have begun preparations towards such a medical breakthrough. For a fee, the bodies of those entertaining such hopes are frozen permanently to await that momentous day. Those who believe that scientists can one day conquer death want us to believe that when such a time arrives, even if we sit in an aeroplane thousands of metres above the surface of the earth and the plane crashes, our bodies will be able to survive.

Chapter 20
A Perfect Scaffold for Support

Have you ever seen pictures suggesting we used to walk on all fours?

I had to learn those theories in school. Though several years ago, though I did not call myself a Christian at that time, the common sense in me told me something could not be true regarding that assertion. Why did we have to walk on all fours in the first place?

How come, I ask myself, have school authorities the world over allowed such an unproven thesis to be thought as fact in our schools? If an uneducated person had propagated such an unproven theory somewhere in one of the poor corners of the universe, hardly anyone would have paid attention to it. On the other hand, because so-called men and women of letters are spreading this lie—men and women boasting qualifications expressed in the letters of the alphabet invented by humankind placed at the end of their names—many have come to believe the lie represents an established fact.

We know that the gorillas in the Congo forest in Africa go on all fours. Why have they not, at least during the last several hundred years, made any physiological advance and evolved further up the ladder into beings capable of walking upright like you and me? Permit me to carry the matter one step further. If evolution, as the name suggests, is not static, why have *we* not been able to develop, for example, feathers, to fly like birds?

The whole world may take me for a naive, crazy person running away from the bare facts. As far as I am concerned, however, the notion that we first walked on all fours is absolute rubbish. The principles of evolution were rubbish at the time King David sang praises to the Lord our shepherd; they were rubbish when the King of Kings and Lord of Lords defeated the grave; they are rubbish today; and they will continue to be rubbish forevermore.

Such a preposterous theory stems from nothing other than unbelief propagated by people who cannot or are not prepared to believe there is a powerful force in the universe, God Almighty, capable of doing anything, and I mean an unqualified anything—no ifs, buts, or perhaps!

Why am I so sure about my stand? The answer is that my Bible tells me Almighty God created me.

"That is a fairy tale!" I hear someone exclaim.

My response is that even should that be the case, and I believe with all my heart it is not, and we decide to discard what the Bible teaches, common sense tells me I am too wonderfully made to have originated from an ape. The German will say, "Punkt, fertig!" The English equivalent, "That's it," in my opinion does not convey the message I want to convey forcefully enough. Punkt, fertig! Yes, that is the end of the matter as far as I am concerned. Nothing will change my stance, and I will hold my position to the end. As I stated before, you may take me to be someone who has gone crazy, someone who is mature for the psychiatric ward.

No bother, that is your opinion and you are welcome to it. It will not change my opinion on the matter one iota. Whom, after all, should I pay allegiance to: the Rock of Ages Cleft for me, or ordinary men and women of flesh?

Someone reading this might well be able to imagine that his or her ancestors might have gone on all fours. Please, please, for heaven's sake, count me out. I do believe with all my heart that at the very, very beginning, Almighty God, the Great Designer, created us to go about our activities in the upright position. To ensure we are able to do so against the force of gravity that He himself had put into place, He decided to put several mechanisms in place in our body. First, He built the human skeletal system as a kind of scaffold that would not only support and protect delicate organs of the body, but also enable us to move from place to place.

I know several people panic at the site of a bare skeleton. But if you have the nerves to do so, you may obtain a plastic reconstruction and spend a few moments reflecting on it. I hope at the end of that period you come to the same conclusion as myself, namely that something is somewhere. I do not think the English translation is able to convey the meaning of what the original Twi *biibi wo baabi* seeks to convey. When the Twi-speaking person says *biibi wo baabi*, the implication is that indeed there is something beyond what you and me are able to see with our naked eyes.

Dear friends, ladies and gentlemen, it is not all science, technology, or expertise. There is indeed something somewhere. If the Divine has not touched you to understand the spiritual dimensions of our existence, my prayer is that Almighty God will reveal Himself to you in His own way.

The world around us, like the human skeleton, points to His existence, but should that not be enough, I sincerely pray Him to visit you in a way He deems fit inasmuch as He appeared to Thomas, the apostle who initially had difficulty believing the Lord's resurrection. I sincerely pray He will appear to you in His own way to enable you to recognise His glory.

I had better return to the main theme of the current presentation before my awe at the incomprehensible authority of the Divine One leads me to swerve permanently from my course.

Let us go back to the skeleton. As I noted, it serves three main purposes: support, protection, and movement. It consists of both fused and individual bones supported and supplemented by ligaments, tendons, muscles, and cartilage.

When we move home, when we transport delicate structures, when we store delicate items at home, we take care to protect them from damage. Some of the methods we apply include covering them with blankets or protective material, putting items in special protective boxes, etc. As an extra precaution, we might write something like, "Fragile: Handle with Care," on the boxes containing the delicate possessions.

In the same way, Almighty God conceived the skeletal system not only to enable us to move from place to place, but to serve as support and protection for some of the delicate organs of the body.

Earlier in this book, we realised how Almighty God chose to place the command centre of our body in a jelly-like substance, the brain. Almighty God did not leave the delicate brain unprotected but placed it in a bony protective cage, the skull. Let us imagine what our lives would be like without a skull to shield our brain from injury.

The football lover that I am, I would not be able to experience the exciting moments associated with goals scored through the powerful headers of some of the brilliant stars of the game were it not for the skull.

So the Creator moulded a protective bony cage, the skull, around the delicate brain. Next, He created openings at suitable locations for important sensory structures such as the eyes, nose, and ears. The skull not only accommodates said organs but also offers them protection.

Another delicate structure that needed protection was the spinal cord, which as we mentioned earlier allows the brain to communicate with other parts of the body. The Creator assigned this function to another component of the skeleton, the spine, a series of vertebrae (backbones) that together form the axis of the skeleton. Together with the ribcage and sternum, the spine also protects the lungs, the heart, and some of the major blood vessels of the body. The skeleton does not only protect some of the delicate organs of the body but provides a framework of support for the body as a whole and helps maintain its shape.

The Creator did not create us to be static, remaining at the same spot from the rising sun to its setting, day after day, week after week, year after year, throughout our stay on earth. He designed the skeleton in such a way as to enable us to move from one place to another.

As a way of facilitating our movement, He inserted joints between bones to serves as levers. Muscles attached to the skeleton by means of tendons facilitate movement. Some of the joints, like the ball and socket joints of the shoulder, allow for a great range of movement, whereas others, like the pivot joint between the neck and the skull, are limited in their movement. To help us maintain equilibrium and not fall over as we move from place to place, He put into place the vestibular system I touched upon earlier on.

As part of our habit of copying or stealing the copyright of Almighty God, some members of our race have come up with a robot. Incredible, the way some of them perform. It is well and good. Yet even the best robot cannot match some of the basic movement coordination of which the human being is capable.

Visit a ballet concert to marvel at the fantastic coordination of the dancers, watch ice-skating either on TV or as a spectator and marvel at the skills of synchronised movement on display. Apart from the instances just mentioned, our skeletal system plays a key role in the production of blood cells. This takes place in the bone marrow.

Before I end my discourse on the skeletal system, I wish to draw attention to another piece of intelligence at work in the way our skeleton is designed. I stated earlier that Almighty God chose to cooperate with humankind in the propagation of our Race via sexual reproduction. The Creator willed it that after conception the unborn child will spend around forty weeks in the womb of the mother to develop into maturity before being born into the world. Because the God I serve does not leave anything to chance, in this case also, He took steps to design the female body in such as way as to enable it to perform the function assigned it. This truth is reflected in the way He designed the female pelvis vis-à-vis that found in the male.

In comparison to the male pelvis, the female pelvis is flatter, more rounded and proportionally larger. The construction leads to both the pelvic inlet and outlet being rounder and larger in the female than in the male. This is necessary to facilitate the passage of the head of the baby in and out of the pelvis during the process of delivery.

Chapter 21
Maintaining Stability in an Ever-Changing World

T he intelligent Designer, God Almighty, placed us on a planet with changing seasons, weather conditions, events, and other challenges. We would expect an intelligent Designer to build into the products of his handiwork the appropriate mechanisms to enable us to adapt to the changing conditions we would face.

As I was about to finish the last paragraph, my computer began to make a funny noise. As I began to wonder what was happening, the reason for the noise flashed through my mind—the intelligent electronic brain behind the computer had envisaged that the device, which had been in operation for a while, would heat to the point where damage might ensue. What was the solution? Answer: Build in a cooling system! The system activate as the temperature of the system begins to approach dangerous levels. The designers placed a type of fan into it to draw air in to cool the system. Engineers at Compaq, Dell, and Siemens may correct me if my information is false.

If the Creator gave the human brain, made of mere soft tissue, the ability to reason, we would naturally expect the Big Boss Himself to be capable of far more intelligence than our brain cells are capable, and be able to fathom mysteries far deeper than we can.

Yet the teeming fans of Charles Darwin, guru of Chance Evolution, expect us to believe our intelligence is the outcome of chance, the products of DNA. When it comes to their own designs and inventions, they expect everyone to stand up and bow their heads in appreciation as their motorcade whisks them to their six-star hotel, where they are refreshed for their appearance before world dignitaries at Humanity's Hall of Fame. They receive their Human Medals of Excellence for discoveries they have made, discoveries supposedly to advance the cause of humankind. Yet who in the end is capable of advancing the cause of humanity but He who Was and Is and Evermore shall be, the King of Kings and Lord of Lords?

As I have reiterated on several occasions during this discourse, contrary to what His enemies, spearheaded by Lucifer the great Deceiver, want the whole world to believe, Someone created the universe, and His name is Almighty God, who is still at the helm of affairs.

To help us maintain a stable milieu within our body system in the presence of ever-changing environmental conditions, Almighty God put into place in our bodies several self-regulatory mechanisms. We could probably ascribe a couple of these to chance, but to give chance credit for the total of the innumerable control mechanisms working in our bodies is to throw common sense to the dogs.

I have touched on, if only briefly, some of these regulatory mechanisms. For example, in the chapter dealing with the heart I mentioned how that fabulous muscular pump is able to adjust its pumping rate to cope with various life situations from the ordinary to the extraordinary, from normal to extreme. Without our heart's ability to stand up to such challenges, hardly any sporting activity would have been possible—neither the game of football (soccer), nor rugby, nor basketball; neither athletics, nor swimming, nor skating. There would be no Olympic games, no American Super Bowl, no Football

World Cup—you name them until the cows come home. It would be a world without sporting activities, and oh, what a world that would be!

The kidney on its part plays a key role to keep the volume of fluid in our body constant. If the kidney worked like a robot, filtering blood and discharging urine at a fixed rate independently of the external circumstances, life would not have been possible. What would, for example, have happened to some members of our race that find no other way to spend their weekends besides engaging in binge drinking, imbibing in the process considerable volumes of beer? They would literally flood their cells with volumes of fluid that in turn would cut short their stay on the planet. Instead of celebrating their weekend, they would in due course find themselves in their graves. In His goodness and kindness, Almighty God endowed the kidney with the capability to adjust its activities to meet the demand of the time.

We have also touched on the interplay between Miss Insulin and her sister Miss Glucagon to maintain a steady glucose level in our body.

I shall consider two regulatory mechanisms in some detail. Have you, once in your lifetime, experienced real danger; a situation that you realised posed a real threat to your life? Perhaps you went to work on your farm in the tropical heat and accidentally stepped on the tail of a python. All of a sudden, the dreadful reptile might have turned and with its eyes glowing as if on fire, took aim at the impudent one that dared cause him pain in that manner. Or perhaps you were on a Safari in Kenya and somehow came in close confrontation with a lion. Or maybe you were walking on the streets of a town when all of a sudden pandemonium broke loose. A gunman had suddenly appeared at one corner brandishing a gun, threatening anyone who did not run away.

Eventually you managed to escape the ordeal. Perhaps you thereafter sat down to ask yourself how you were able to mobilise the spurt of energy that enabled you to escape the life-threatening situation. How could someone who under normal circumstances would probably have been beaten in a race against a tortoise, manage to generate sufficient energy to spring from the danger zone in barely any time at all? With danger out of sight, you begin to regret you did not have a stopwatch at that fateful moment to record your speed. What a missed opportunity! You may well have broken a world record for running the one hundred metres.

I read the other day of instances in which mothers have been able to lift cars off their trapped children. Such unusual feats of strength are typical examples of the so-called "fight and flight" mechanism placed in us by Almighty God to help us escape or fight dangers that threatens our lives or those of others. I shall give a short account of how the mechanism works.

Adrenaline, a substance in our body, plays a key role in the execution of the escape mechanism. Let us take the example of the mother confronted with the scene of her child trapped under a vehicle. In a twinkle of an eye the Commander-in-Charge of her forces, Lt. General Brain, issues a Red Alarm to General Adrenalin. Immediately, the General activates the Priority One Emergency code of the body defences. This results in frenetic activity inside the body. Among other things, the heart begins immediately to increase its pumping activity aimed at supplying additional blood to the muscles. To enable additional blood to reach the muscles in time, the vessels supplying blood to the muscle widen. The bronchioles, the tiny air-filled spaces in the lungs directly involved in exchange of air in the lungs, dilate to allow the increased flow of oxygen to enter the body—oxygen needed to burn additional energy to support the increased muscular activity.

Extra glucose needed to meet an increased energy demand of the muscles is also mobilised from the liver and elsewhere and sent to the muscles. It is the resulting spurt of energy that will enable the mother, who in normal situations would never dream of attempting to lift an object as heavy as a car, to do exactly that in that extraordinary circumstance.

Finally, I want to touch briefly on the mechanisms at work in us to regulate body temperature. As we were told in the science class of the of the U.S. high school during our earlier visit, mammals, the group to which human beings are classified, need to maintain a constant body temperature to survive on earth. How do they do so on a planet that can be as hot as the Sahara and as cold as the Arctic? God assigned the responsibility of maintaining bodily temperature within a realm conducive to life to an area in our brain known as the hypothalamus. The hypothalamus is responsible not only for the maintenance of a constant body temperature but several other regulatory functions in the body. It is indeed clever in its activities. In the matter of temperature control, this is how it goes about matters:

To begin, it sets a core body temperature of about thirty-seven degrees Celsius. Having decided on that figure, the hypothalamus goes to great extents to maintain that temperature. How does it achieve that in a world of changing environmental temperatures? Well, it makes use of agents or thermoregulatory effectors in place in several parts of the body.

Some of the receptors are located in internal organs and structures such as the spinal cord, digestive tract, great veins and hypothalamus. Others are in place within the skin. The temperature sentinels in the body do not sleep while on guard duty like human sentinels are inclined to do, but instead they maintain vigilance around the clock. They are, if you like, spies for the hypothalamus, relaying to the boss on a regular basis the temperature prevailing outside of the command centre.

When we enter a cold air-conditioned room, temperature receptors detect the changed circumstance immediately. Immediately, the information travels to the hypothalamus. The chief temperature regulator identifies an imminent threat to the body's core temperature and goes into action to activate a response mechanism aimed at heat conservation. First, it signs a decree to order the vessels supplying blood to the skin to immediately constrict or reduce their size and, in doing so, decrease blood flow to the skin, which in turn prevents the loss of heat to the outside.

If it deems it necessary, the hypothalamus initiates other measures aimed at maintaining a stable temperature. It could cause the secretion of hormones such as thyroxin and adrenaline, which in turn could lead to increased cell activity aimed ultimately at increased heat production. Furthermore, the heat regulator could command the muscles to begin shivering and in the process produce heat to help raise the body temperature.

The opposite happens in a hot condition, when the body needs to cool down. In this case, too, temperature sentinels dutifully relay the message to the temperature regulator. This time, the regulator authorises the vessels to open to allow heat to escape. The sweat glands in the skin are also charged to begin sweat production. As the sweat evaporates from the surface of the skin, it utilises heat from the skin, which in turn has a cooling effect on our body.

We notice in the above control mechanisms how much order and discipline is at work in our body. Children may neglect parents' instructions; soldiers may occasionally refuse to obey the order of superiors. It is not so in the case of the command structure in place in our body. The order goes out from the hypothalamus to the body to take steps towards heat production, and so it happens. We ourselves have the tendency to say things like, "This is my body, this is my life," though we do not even control the control mechanism of the hypothalamus.

Who among us for example has been able to prevent muscles from shivering? Who among us has been able, once, to prevent body sweating? On certain occasions, we feel uncomfortable when we begin to sweat. For example, when we are sitting before a panel at an interview for a job for which we highly yearn, or when we sit before a panel of examiners, we wish we could postpone our sweating in order not to betray to the outside world that we are burning within ourselves.

"Throw your feelings to the dogs!" Your hypothalamus may tell you. It has the Divine order to make sure your body temperature remains within a range needed to keep you alive. And since the Divine has given it the responsibility so to do, it must act accordingly— whether you think you arrived here by chance or not.

Yes, the hypothalamus, having had its contract of engagement signed in heaven, has no other option than to obey to the letter the duty assigned it by the Most High.

Chapter 22
Adam and Eve Supplementing Each Other

O ur discourse began with the conception of an individual. The sexual act had taken place and the sperm of the male had penetrated the egg of the female to form the union that would develop into a human being. I shall end this discourse by returning to this issue.

As I said at the beginning, Almighty Father of heaven and earth could have come up with a system for propagating the human race based on asexual reproduction, as it occurs in certain lower organisms. In organisms such as bacteria and fungi, the individual breaks up from time to time into two equal parts. The Divine command could have reached me, the poor subsistence farmer's son at my little village in Ghana, to break up into two or three or four individuals as the Divine deemed fit. Since the command would have originated from God Almighty, Creator of heaven and earth, so would it have come to pass, for what is my body to resist the decree of the most Powerful Force in the entire universe?

Human faculties may not be in a position to figure out how exactly this system of human multiplication would have functioned, but since the Almighty Father has the power and ability to do whatever He chooses, He would have found a way to make the system work.

You and I may consider the idea bizarre, but the Great Designer could have made use of the freedom He as Designer had to implement a single parent model. This model differs from the one we refer to today when marriages break down and one parent assumes the responsibility of raising the children that came out of the union. The type of single parent model I have in mind would have been truly original.

We could refer to it as the one-man-thousand solution. One might wonder what the term one-man-thousand implies. In my native Ghana, we use it to describe a situation whereby one person tries to be all-in-all. Take the surgery, or practice, of our family doctor as an example. Our GP sits at the reception to register the patients that arrive, fishes their files from the cabinet, and carries out routine checks for their body temperature, blood pressure, weight, and height before inviting them to the consulting room to take their history and examine them. The doctor would lead them to the dispensary to dispense the prescribed medication before finally seeing them off at the exit. It is a modern-day version of Robinson Crusoe, if you like.

Indeed, with our limited faculties, we may not be able to comprehend fully how things would have worked out, but God Almighty could well have chosen to equip the first human being Adam with both organs needed for sexual reproduction.

Such a solution would have saved married couples the world over some of the problems that have simmered in their homes in the past. It would have saved them the problems that continue to simmer in their homes as I write, and which will continue to simmer in their homes as long as life exists, not to mention the millions of divorce hearings that would have been avoided annually worldwide.

One particular group of professionals would not find that prospect humorous, though. I have in mind the vast number of solicitors worldwide who earn their daily bread from the booming divorce industry.

As we know from the Holy Bible, God Almighty settled on a different model: "And the Lord God said, it is not good that the man should be alone; I will make him an help meet for him" (Gen. 2:18). This leads me to think the main reason Almighty God settled for the present model was companionship. He ordained Adam and Eve to become companions, each for the other. This also led me to conclude that Almighty God did not divine that we should live isolated lives. Our so-called civilisation has led to the individualisation of society, with the result that many today are living isolated lives, dying of boredom. That, however, forestalls the area of our present discussion.

He who is the Big Boss over everything seen and unseen decided in the end to create two different sexes of the human family to complement each other in marriage.

These days a lot of talk goes on in regard to the equality of sexes. In that, there exists a broad range of issues to address. It is not the remit of this book to begin a debate on that matter. The fact remains, however, that whatever we as humans, through legislation, seek to achieve by way of equality of the sexes, anatomically, the Creator divined that we should be male and female. While making us equal by virtue of our common humanity, He created us different by virtue of our differing sexual functions. So it is and so it will remain till the end of time.

Those who believe in chance evolution may not have any problem with regard to the extent to which the beautiful concept of human sexuality has become defiled and degraded. What else can one expect from people who, inspired by their atheistic worldview, live in line with the thinking, "Let us eat and drink for tomorrow we die"? If life came about by chance and has no meaning, if it ends at the grave, let us make the best of it while it is day. Let us consume as much food and drink as we can, exchange as many sexual partners as we can; indeed, let us have as much fun as we can so long as we have breath.

I will not hesitate to declare in the mighty name of the Lord of Hosts that no matter how much effort ordinary mortals might invest in spreading falsehoods concerning how the universe came into being, the fact remains that, "In the beginning God created the heaven and the earth" (Gen. 1:1). That is the truth and the whole truth, valid yesterday, today, and forever.

Concerning human sexuality, the Creator, having decided on a male-female solution, placed the appropriate mechanism in place to ensure His perfect will and perfect world would be fulfilled.

I am neither an engineer nor a designer, so those of you who read what I am about to write may wish to send a note of protest to me if I am spreading a falsehood.

Let us assume an organization will erect two spacious tents for a public event. Let us assume that to motivate the volunteers who have sacrificed their time and energy to help put up the structures, the local authority decides to award a prize to the group that finishes first. Let us suppose all agreed at outset that iron bars would support the tent. The builders knew the respective sizes of the steel rods meant to support the construction. Somehow, probably as result of memory lapse, both groups distorted the information supplied. Based on wrong information, the first group dug round holes, each measuring 10 cm in diameter into which to fix the rods. Soon a truck arrives to deliver the building material. As it turns out, the rods measure 15 cm in diameter instead of 10 cm. The group begins to panic, for there is little time left to complete the assignment. Initially they resort to brute force in the attempt to fix the oversize rods into the holes, to no avail. In the end, they have no other option than to enlarge the original holes.

As the members of the above group are coming to terms with the thought of finishing far behind their counterparts, word reaches them that the other group are not faring any better. Though they got the message right with regard to the form and size of the rods, they received rectangular rods instead of round ones. These turned out to be too big to fix into the circular holes. Confusion abounds as the organisers make frantic efforts to get things done in time for the event that will begin shortly.

Now, from what we know of the female and male organs of reproduction, does it not amount to blatant disrespect to God Almighty to assume we could be the product of chance evolution? How, for heaven's sake, can anyone in control of common sense arrive at such a conclusion?

Let us sit down to ponder this. Is it not an affront on the dignity of Almighty God that we have the audacity to teach our schoolchildren what we have so far been teaching them, namely that we arrived here by way of chance evolution with the aid of its cousins natural selection and mutation? Mutation followed by natural selection is nonsense. Can chance design a male sexual organ to fit exactly into a female sexual organ? Can chance cause sperm production by a male to fertilise an egg and thereafter cause the fertilised egg to implant on the walls of the womb where it will develop into maturity? Can chance cause the matured individual to be born at the right time and cause the mother's breast to produce milk at the right moment for breastfeeding? The idea is simply outrageous! As far as I am concerned, anyone who denies the existence of God should be barred from assuming any office that carries substantial responsibility. How can anyone who has thrown common sense to the dogs be able to pass responsible judgment?

As I mentioned, Almighty God, having willed that reproduction would be by means of two individuals complementing each other, put the right mechanism in place to ensure that was the case. First, He designed the male and female sexual organs to fit each other. He did not aim to place a rectangular bar in a round hole; neither did He think of putting a cube in a triangle.

The Great Designer, making use of the artistic freedom that is His privilege as a Designer, decreed that the body makes the sperm of the male within a temperature range below that of the human body. Having decided that, He took the necessary steps to ensure that indeed was the case by placing the testis, the factory where the sperm are produced, outside the body of the male, where the temperature is usually below that persisting in the body.

Having willed that the unborn child should develop deep in the body of the woman, the Creator faced the problem of how to get the sperm of the male to travel that distance to bring about fertilisation. In our day, we are busy stealing the copyright of God Almighty without His permission. One way we do that is by way of in vitro fertilisation of the egg and sperm—IVF for short. It would be better if only, after we have done so, we would give honour where honour is due. Instead, many of our race, after they have copied the technology of Almighty God, go about bragging, claiming the title of mini-gods for themselves. I am not implying that I do not recognise the joy the technology has brought into the hearts of many worldwide. However, we must learn to keep matters in the right perspective. Sometimes, some Gurus in the field create the impression that humanity might have ceased to multiply without their gracious intervention.

Almighty God could have set the table for the male and female, but if they had no appetite for the meal, what would have happened? Indeed, if after the Almighty God had created male and the female they had repulsed each other instead of being attracted, what use would that have been to His plan of sexual reproduction? It is superfluous to begin a lecture on the matter of female and male attraction,

132

considering the volume of poems, verses, and songs that both sexes have over the several centuries written in adoration and worship of each other. Perhaps someone came up with the term "woman power" in considering the influence the mystifying female charm could have on the reasoning of males.

God designed female and male to attract each other. That would still not have meant much, as mere attraction would not have resulted in the sperm of the male fertilising the egg of the female. So the Great Designer sat down to consider how He could overcome the hurdle— namely, to get the sperm of the male from the comfort of the hotel room in testis to travel deep into the body of the female to fertilise the egg. In the end, He designed a male sexual organ that would be best suited for the job. In my opinion, the Creator had two options to consider as He worked to design the male sexual organ: create an organ in a permanently erected state or devise a mechanism that could well be termed "erection on demand."

Contemplate for a moment a world made up of several million males going about with erected sexual organs. In His great wisdom, the Great Designer decided to settle for the erection-on-demand model. It is not within the realm of this book to delve into any detail with regard to the complex mechanism He put in place to ensure an erection in the male. Here I will provide only a brief overview.

First, Almighty God built the sexual organ of the male as two chambers. As a next step, He filled the chambers with a spongy tissue known as *corpora canernosa*, within which are muscles, fibrous tissues, spaces, veins, and arteries.

He then wrapped the spongy chambers in a thick membrane called the *tunica albuginea*. To facilitate the communication of the rod-like object with the outside world, the Great Designer bored a tunnel through the underside of the organ to serve not only as a route for the sperm on their mission to fertilise the egg, but also as a passage for urine on its journey to the outside of the body.

Sensory and mental stimulation trigger the erection process. Several body parts work together to ensure it works. In the first place, the brain sends a message of sexual arousal through the nervous system to the male sexual organ. This message causes the muscles of the *corpora cavernosa* to relax. At the same time, the size of the artery, the vessel carrying blood from the heart to supply the organ, expands to twice its original size. As a result, the volume of blood it carries increases to about sixteen times what it once was.

If only the matter would end there! But no, the Great Designer took further steps to ensure the desired effect was achieved, namely the stiffening and enlargement of the male sexual organ to facilitate sperm transport to the female. Consequently, at the same time the blood supply to the male sexual organ has increased tremendously, the command reaches the veins, the vessels responsible for transporting blood, to block all passages leading away from it. The blood cannot escape. The *tunica albuginea*, the thick wall wrapped around the *corpora cavernosa*, also plays an important role in helping to trap the blood and in so doing sustain the erection.

It is astounding, the incredible intelligence Almighty God placed in various organs and systems in our body to ensure His plans for His creation remain intact.

As I said earlier, after Almighty God says A, He goes on to say B and C until his word has accomplished what He set out to achieve. In line with His nature, He put mechanisms in place to ensure the process of erection reverses after a while. The process begins with the contraction of the muscles of the organ. This reduces the inflow of blood to the levels that persisted before the erection process. Simultaneously, the blockage on the walls of the veins lifts to allow outflow of blood.

It is one thing to have an erected male organ that can penetrate the body of the female; it is another to get the sperm sleeping comfortably in the luxury hotel of the testicles to travel the considerable distance into the womb of the female and fertilise the egg released there. The Great Designer, the I Am That I Am, as usual, had a solution to the problem. In the process of orgasm and ejaculation, He placed a powerful mechanism in place in the male to help propel the sperm forcefully into the womb of the female.

What you are about to read is my own hypothesis concerning the matter of human sexual reproduction; you may choose to accept or discard it.

I think the Creator, after He pronounced His judgement on Eve following the fall soon became aware of the inconveniences that would become associated with sexual reproduction as applied to humans. "Unto the woman he said, I will greatly multiply thy sorrow and thy conception; in sorrow thou shalt bring forth children; and thy desire [shall be] to thy husband, and he shall rule over thee" (Gen. 3:16).

First, there was the burden on the woman of her having to carry the unborn child approximately forty long weeks in her body. Second was the sorrow or pain she would experience in childbirth. Third was the headache, particularly for the mother and to some extent the father, associated with caring for the new addition to the family. Those who have gone through the experience do not need me to lecture them on the challenges this responsibility entails, especially during the initial stages—the yelling of a hungry child, the need to wash the baby regularly, the sleepless nights.

In considering the above, the Almighty might have concluded that unless He placed some reward mechanism in place in the project, humanity that had a short while earlier demonstrated its spirit of rebellion in concrete terms, could, in this matter, also decide not to cooperate with Him. Consequently, He decided to give the whole process a certain degree of excitement and pleasure.

Having had the privilege to witness a few childbirths myself is the only reason I can explain why mothers, after they have gone through the ordeal of childbirth once, voluntarily subject themselves to the agonising experience repeatedly.

Of course, Almighty God who knows the beginning from the end was with all certainty aware that the gratification aspect of His project would be subject to abuse by the sometimes naughty, other moments tricky, and yet other times rebellious beings into whose hands He decided to entrust dominion over His creation. Yet for reasons known to Him, He decided to go ahead with the venture.

As I mentioned at the outset, this is a hypothesis originating from the Department of Fantasy of my own naughty brain. You may assign it to the waste bin if you do not find it palatable or convincing.

What makes the whole concept of sexual reproduction amazing and mind-boggling is the interplay put in place by the Creator to ensure the attainment of the goal envisaged. How, for example, would an offspring emerge from the coming together of male and female should the sperm introduced into the body of the female not meet with a corresponding Princess Egg whose heart is burning for her Prince? Conversely, what would it profit the Princess Egg the female released if her Prince did not arrive at the right time to cause the execution of the union? As the saying goes, it takes two to tango.

That brings me to another aspect of human sexual reproduction, namely the female menstrual cycle. Before I proceed, bear with me for a short digression.

The proponents of evolution have sought to reduce God's creation to the molecular level. Being able to understand the architecture of the gene, they go about asking us to rise up, lift them, and carry them on our shoulders on a triumphal march through the cities of the world.

Humankind has been able to encode the human genome. And so what, dear friends? Will that knowledge lead us to conquer death or prevent the next earthquake or tsunami from striking?

That is not to say I am praying for the next disaster to smash us. I am just trying to draw our attention to how powerless we are before the forces at work in God's universe. Who are we to boast of anything, brothers and sisters, let alone create the impression of being able to challenge Almighty God? We have cracked the human genome, we have super brains, and everything depends on us, on our technology, on technological progress! Your brains! What are your brains before He who placed that jelly-like structure into your skull in the first place?

The question to consider at the outset is why there is a need for a menstrual cycle in the first place. As I mentioned, Almighty God decided to cooperate with humankind in the propagation of the human race. In His wisdom, He decided on the principle of division of labour, assigning the male and the female different functions of sexual reproduction. Among other things, He assigned the female the role of carrying the individual resulting from the union of the egg and the sperm and providing the child the opportunity to develop and grow in her womb until such time that the baby will be capable of surviving under the conditions on earth.

To facilitate the performance of the role assigned to her, Almighty God instituted the female menstrual cycle. In our present discussion, we will assume an average duration of twenty-eight days, although it may deviate a few days from individual to individual.

The cycle in effect is the female body's way of preparing itself to accommodate the individual who will result from a union between Mr. Sperm and Miss Egg. I will begin with day one of the cycle, the day on which the menstrual bleeding sets in. For the female experiencing it for the first time, it is an indication of coming of age, of being, theoretically capable of carrying a baby in the womb. For the female who is not experiencing it for the first time, it is an indication that fertilisation did not take place during the previous cycle. The explanation for the bleeding is the following: during the days preceding the event, the womb made extensive preparation towards providing a home for the would-be product of the union referred to above. The expected union not having materialised, the womb decides, albeit with a heavy heart, to discard the material put in place to receive the newcomer.

We may compare the situation to an occasion where we have used our most precious bed sheet and pillowcase to set the bed in the guestroom of our home in anticipation of a most honoured guest. Just as we are expecting the arrival, we receive a call saying that circumstances beyond control had forced our guest to postpone the trip. Disappointed, we undress the bed to await a possible visit in the future.

We might well compare the situation to the bridegroom who orders delicious food from the most famous restaurant in town and who has set the table at home to host a wedding reception after the exchange of rings at the city hall. At the last minutes, after the presiding officer had gone through all the formalities and requested the bride to say yes to her prince, she declares to the bewilderment of her would-be husband and the invited guests that she is not in a position to do so. Disappointed and burning with rage, the bridegroom hurries home and throws the good-looking meal into the dustbin.

Depending on the individual involved, the menstrual bleeding may last anywhere between three and seven days (or more). When the bleeding is over, the brain sends instructions to a structure located at its base, the pituitary gland, to begin releasing into the bloodstream a hormone it had all along been producing and storing in its body. This hormone on its part carries the name *follicle-stimulating hormone*, or

FSH. FSH in turn instructs one of the two ovaries of the womb to order one of the several follicles it is harbouring to grow into maturity. The follicles are tiny liquid-filled sacs, each containing an egg. At birth, each girl already has several follicles. They remain dormant until she reaches maturity.

Usually during each menstrual cycle, only one follicle grows into maturity. In rare instances, however, two or more may do so simultaneously and release their eggs into the womb. There are two ovaries on each side of the womb. For the sake of fairness, the follicles release at alternating months from each ovary.

Prior to the release of the matured egg into the womb, the maturing follicle releases a considerable amount of a hormone known as *oestrogen* into the bloodstream. Under the influence of oestrogen, the lining of the womb grows increasingly thicker. Just about the middle of the 28-day cycle, that is, round about the fourteenth day, the matured egg drops into the womb. We call this event *ovulation*.

The important role the follicle plays does not end with ovulation. Now re-christened *corpus luteum*, it begins to produce, in addition to oestrogen, another hormone, progesterone, into the bloodstream. Together, both hormones support and maintain the thickened walls of the uterus in anticipation of the possible implantation of the fertilised egg within it.

In the absence of fertilisation, the corpus luteum degenerates in about fourteen days. With decreasing levels of oestrogen and progesterone in the bloodstream brought about by the degeneration of the corpus luteum, a new menstrual cycle soon sets in.

Ladies and gentlemen of the jury, I invite you to join me in pondering over another aspect of Divine ingenuity surrounding sexual reproduction. Almighty God, aware that He had placed only one womb at the disposal of the female, and that the womb can cope with only one pregnancy at a time, put a mechanism in place to prevent a woman who is already nourishing a pregnancy from conceiving another child during the period.

Yes, Almighty God was aware of the burden placed on the woman by a child. Even during the period when she carries a seed, the likelihood is that Mr. Male will not leave her alone even though she is already anguishing under the burden of the seed she is carrying. She is barely able to rest in peace when she retires to rest after a busy day's activities. Yet, as is his custom, her husband may get on her nerves not only by way of his snores, but also in various aspects of their relationship. Realizing this eventuality, the Almighty Father, Creator of the atheist as well as those who believe in Him, placed a mechanism in place in the female to prevent her from releasing an egg throughout the period she is carrying a seed.

Who are you, champion of chance evolution, to challenge the wisdom of the Creator of the whole universe? Indeed, who are you, the tiny spot that you are, before the omnipotent, omnipresent God? Whom do you think you are, mere mortal that you are, before Him who commands immense powers and empowers your brain, made up of mere jelly-like matter that barely has the ability to fathom the infinite mind? Who are you, friend? Who are you, brother? Who are you, sister? You are nothing before the Omnipotent. I exhort you to be careful, friend, and you, brother, and you, sister—you who go about spreading malicious lies about the Lord of Hosts. If indeed you have wisdom, I advise you to take lessons from the fate of Sodom and Gomorrah!

Almighty God took yet further steps to protect the new mother. Aware of the enormous strain that would be placed on her by her new arrival on earth, the Creator instituted a plan aimed at spacing the period between the births of her children. We may call it Divine Family Planning. There is indeed amazing wisdom behind the concept. First, He empowered the female breast to produce milk to feed the

SEEING GOD THROUGH THE HUMAN BODY

baby. Next, He entrusted the very hormone that would oversee the production of milk, giving it the responsibility of preventing the body from producing the chemicals that could initiate the growth of the follicle in the ovary that could lead to ovulation. In other words, as long as the mother is breastfeeding her child, ovulation does not occur.

Let us consider the plan in practical terms. In so doing, let us take the case of a mother breastfeeding her baby over a period of twelve months. That would usually imply that over that period she would not likely become pregnant. Let us assume that she becomes pregnant not long after she has stopped breastfeeding. That would imply there would be approximately two-year interval between the children. For those mothers who breastfeed for a longer period, the spacing of births could be longer.

Chapter 23
We Are Fearfully and Wonderfully Made

꒜

I have come to the end of my discourse. What you have learned about the human body, mind you, is only a brief overview of the topic. Indeed, dwelling on the fine details of how God builds the human body and how it functions would require volumes.

The human body, without exaggeration, is a miracle. Better still, it is the sum total of miracles. Indeed, there are thousands upon thousands, if not millions upon millions or billions upon billions, of miracles simultaneously at work in our body to keep us going.

"I will praise thee; for I am fearfully and wonderfully made: marvellous are thy works; and that my soul knoweth right well" (Ps. 139:14).

Without exaggeration, we *are* fearfully and wonderfully made. Because our Creator invested so much intelligence into our body, the doctors who take it upon themselves to help us when something goes wrong have realised they cannot deal with the matter unless they break things into specialties. I do not want to bore you unnecessarily with a list of all the departments of medicine. Still, to help you appreciate the immense power and intelligence of He who designed our body, I shall list some of the fields, or departments, of medicine.

We may list the departments in alphabetical order: A for Anatomy, B for Biochemistry, C for Chemical Pathology, D for Dermatology, E for ENT (Ear Nose and Throat), G for Gynaecology and Gastroenterology; H for Human Genetics, I for Internal Medicine, M for Maxillofacial, Microbiology, Medicine, and Maternity Care; N for Nephrology, Neurology, Neurosurgery, and Neonatology; O for Oncology, Orthopaedic Science, and Ophthalmology; P for Psychiatry, R for Rheumatology, S for Surgery, T for Transplant Medicine, U for Urology, and V for Virology.

Consider the large number of fields of medicine needed to treat the bodies of Adam and Eve gone wrong. Mind you, that list is by no means complete.

I do believe God Almighty created us instantaneously. Yet there is so much intelligence and wisdom built into us that several specialities of medicine rather than a handful are required to try to sort out things when things go wrong.

With this in mind, please join me in one last reflection before we finally close the chapter on this book. Indeed, we will have to do so at a certain stage, for unless we do so we could find enough reason to ponder over the Might of the Lord Zebaoth indefinitely.

Almighty God is not only a Powerful Creator; He is also the Greatest Physician of all time. It should not surprise anyone that He who created us must also be in a position to repair our bodies when things go wrong.

What a huge difference between His healing powers and that of ordinary mortal man. Whereas human physicians need to specialise in a field of medicine to cope with the immense challenge, the Great Physician does not!

More strikingly, He does not need the techniques of conventional medicine in His activities—no clinical examinations, no X-rays, no MRI-scans, no CT-scans.

His healing powers know no bounds. Let us consider the patient paralysed from the waist downward—perhaps a road traffic accident resulted in the spinal cord being torn apart. As much as medical science will want to help the young lady, a mother of two young children, regain her ability to walk, they realise that based on the knowledge of modern medical practice, there is nothing they can do to help her walk.

Then enter King Jesus Christ, the Son of the Living God, Creator of heaven and earth. What does He do? He pats the patient on the shoulder and with a voice full of authority, issues the command: "Young lady, get up and walk!"

Instantaneously, a new spinal cord replaces the broken cord in her body. Not only that, but her muscles, weakened through months of disuse, regain their vitality. Moments later the lady, minutes earlier confined to her wheelchair, runs about wildly, shouting on top of her voice and giving glory to the Lord of creation for the supernatural intervention in her life.

The Lord of creation moves on. He spots a blind man whose loving and caring wife is leading him. She has stood by him since the time a chemical accident at the factory caused him blindness in both eyes. As much as medical science tried to help him, his eyesight would not return. At that moment, the Lord of creation passes by. He asks husband and wife to stop for a while. He then moves to the blind man and stretches his right hand towards him. Without even touching him, both eyes, dissolved in their sockets by the aggressive acid, instantaneously reform. That is not the end of the story—the scars in his face resulting from the accident become skin as soft as that of a newborn baby.

Finally, the Lord of creation arrives at the scene of a severe accident. A crowd has gathered. We can see flashing lights from the vehicles of both the police and the paramedics called to the scene even from a distance. The paramedics are carrying the mortal remains of a middle-aged man on a stretcher into their vehicle. The victim had earlier fallen a considerable distance from a building under construction, his body landing on the hard ground. So ferocious was the fall that his skull shattered into pieces causing his brain to gush out of his body.

Even as He is some distance away from the scene, the Angel of Death recognises the King of Kings and takes to his heels. King Jesus orders the paramedics to stand still. After initially expressing their reservations, they heed the call of the Stranger.

"Get up and return to your wife and four children, friend!" He who overcame death on the cross of Calvary centuries ago speaks into the ears of the dead. Immediately the disfigured brain of the victim returns to its original size. The blood in his body, almost completely lost due to the fall, returns, and the heart begins pumping blood to perfuse his organs. At the same time, the breathing mechanism springs into action.

The avowed adherents of atheism, the gurus in the matters of chance evolution and natural selection, on hearing about the incredible things happening around them, decide to call an emergency conference to deliberate on the issues, to seek scientific explanations for the awe-inspiring miracles of our Lord. Sadly, these fans of Charles Darwin and those the world over are losing their own lives, dying without the promise and assurance of salvation, of everlasting life, whilst holding high the banner of atheism, for they are too preoccupied with fishing out explanations to explain the unusual phenomena of God's healing power.

Meanwhile, He who is and was and evermore shall be continues His journey through the world, looking out for those ready to open their hearts and minds to accept Him, those who are ready to depend on common sense and accept the fact of the creation of the world by God Almighty.